T0323944

"Nurses are not just the backbone of healthcare; they are the trailblazers in the 'ecosystem transformation' that AI-based informatics promises. Their hands-on patient care, both within and beyond the traditional healthcare system, is set to experience a paradigm shift akin to the Galileo-Copernicus revolution in science. As a physician leader, former CEO, and a thought leader in US Health Policy across three administrations, I am convinced that the integration of Large Language Models in healthcare, championed by nursing leadership, will mark a defining moment in medical history. 'Empowering Nurses with Technology' is a vital manual that equips nurses to spearhead this innovation, ensuring exemplary patient care and safety."

Dr. Jim Weinstein, VP, Microsoft

"Today, nursing informatics is at a critical inflexion point. Key technologies that once helped launch the specialty continue to evolve, yet at the same time, new innovations are rapidly gaining traction. Thus, the knowledge and expertise of nurse informaticists and other health IT professionals must rapidly evolve as well. The strategies outlined in this book are key to ensuring that new capabilities such as artificial intelligence and precision health are wisely implemented and carefully managed to realize the benefits and ensure that patient care is not compromised by their use. This book is an essential resource for equipping informatics experts and their partners as they guide the nursing workforce in understanding and embracing this exciting new evolution in technology."

Joyce Sensmeier MS, RN-BC, FHIMSS, FAAN,
Senior Advisor HIMSS (retired)

"'Empowering Nurses with Technology: A Practical Guide to Nurse Informatics' is a comprehensive and timely resource for nurses navigating the rapidly evolving healthcare technology landscape.

This 10-chapter book covers crucial topics in health informatics, from the fundamentals to cutting-edge applications. The text expertly explores electronic health records and their impact on clinical decision-making, providing nurses with practical insights for leveraging these tools effectively.

It delves into artificial intelligence and clinical decision support systems, equipping readers with knowledge to harness these technologies for improved patient care. Chapters on telehealth, telemedicine, and mobile health initiatives offer valuable guidance for nurses adapting to remote care delivery models. The book also addresses critical ethical and legal considerations in nursing informatics, ensuring readers are prepared to navigate complex issues in this digital age.

With its focus on training and education, this guide is an excellent resource for nursing students and practicing professionals seeking to enhance their informatics competencies.

By exploring the future of nursing informatics, the book prepares readers for upcoming technological advancements and their potential impact on healthcare delivery.

This practical guide is essential for nurses looking to thrive in the technology-driven healthcare environment, offering a perfect blend of foundational knowledge and forward-thinking insights."

Marion J. Ball EdD, FLHIMSS, FCHIME, FAAN, FACMIExecutive Director of the Multi-Interprofessional Center for Health Informatics University of Texas, Arlington (retired)

"Healthcare is built on the foundations of collaborative communities. Working together allows us to deliver services and strive for better outcomes. In this book, Dr. Kathleen McGrow helps us understand how we can evolve as individuals and teams using the latest technology and harnessing the power of ever-increasing data. Writing from her own experiences as a clinician and long-time technology leader, the approach is uniquely practical whilst ensuring that patients are kept at the centre as this new field of informatics empowers us to do more. I highly recommend this book to both nurses looking to grow their own knowledge and those working alongside them who can sense the opportunity in health technology brings."

Dr Umang Patel, CCIO Microsoft & NHS Paediatrician

"'Empowering Nurses with Technology: A Practical Guide to Nurse Informatics' is an indispensable resource for modern healthcare professionals. This comprehensive guide navigates the complexities of health information systems, providing clear insights into how seamless data sharing can enhance patient care and operational efficiency. One of the standout features of this book is its exploration of artificial intelligence (AI) in healthcare. The author demystifies AI, highlighting its potential to revolutionize diagnostics, treatment plans, and patient monitoring. Additionally, the sections on telehealth and mHealth are particularly timely, offering practical advice on leveraging these technologies to expand access to care and enhance patient engagement. It empowers the nurse to engage with data at a deeper level. Overall, 'Empowering Nurses with Technology' is a great read for those looking to stay ahead in the rapidly evolving field of nurse informatics."

Barbara Van de Castle DNP, RN, NI-BC
Assistant Professor at University of Maryland
School of Nursing

Empowering Nurses with Technology

Nursing informatics is the specialty that integrates nursing science with multiple information management and analytical sciences to identify, define, manage, and communicate data, information, knowledge, and wisdom in nursing practice. It allows nurses to deliver evidence-based and patient-centered care, improve human health, and advance medical research. It also enhances clinical workflows so that nurses and other personnel can care for patients more efficiently and effectively.

Some of the benefits of nursing informatics include a reduction in medical errors, lowered costs, improved nurse productivity, and better care coordination among nurses, physicians, pharmacists, and others throughout various care stages. *Empowering Nurses with Technology: A Practical Guide to Nurse Informatics* is a comprehensive guidebook for nurses and healthcare professionals looking to understand the role of technology in modern nursing practices. This book covers the basics of healthcare technology, including electronic health records (EHRs), telehealth, and mobile health applications. This book offers practical advice for implementing technology in nursing workflows, as well as strategies for training and engaging nursing staff in the use of new technology. It also explores the impact of technology on patient care and outcomes, discussing topics such as patient safety, privacy, and data security.

This book provides a useful resource for nurses seeking to leverage technology to improve the quality and efficiency of their care while also enhancing their professional development and job satisfaction.

Empowering Nurses with Technology

A Practical Guide to Nurse Informatics

Kathleen McGrow

Routledge
Taylor & Francis Group

NEW YORK AND LONDON

Designed cover image: Shutterstock

First published 2025
by Routledge
605 Third Avenue, New York, NY 10158

and by Routledge
4 Park Square, Milton Park, Abingdon, Oxon, OX14 4RN

Routledge is an imprint of the Taylor & Francis Group, an informa business

© 2025 Kathleen McGrow

The right of Kathleen McGrow to be identified as author of this work has been asserted in accordance with sections 77 and 78 of the Copyright, Designs and Patents Act 1988.

All rights reserved. No part of this book may be reprinted or reproduced or utilised in any form or by any electronic, mechanical, or other means, now known or hereafter invented, including photocopying and recording, or in any information storage or retrieval system, without permission in writing from the publishers.

Trademark notice: Product or corporate names may be trademarks or registered trademarks, and are used only for identification and explanation without intent to infringe.

ISBN: 9781032575124 (hbk)
ISBN: 9781032575100 (pbk)
ISBN: 9781003439721 (ebk)

DOI: 10.4324/9781003439721

Typeset in Garamond
by Newgen Publishing UK

To all the nurses and nurse informaticists,
this book is dedicated to you, the unsung heroes of
healthcare. Your tireless efforts, compassion, and dedication
to patient care are the heartbeat of our healthcare system.
You are the ones who are there at every step of the patient
journey, providing comfort, care, and understanding.

To the nurse informaticists, who bridge the gap between
technology and patient care, your work is invaluable. You
are the architects of the digital transformation in healthcare,
ensuring that technology serves the needs of patients and
nurses alike. Your expertise empowers nurses to deliver the
best possible care, making healthcare safer, more efficient,
and more effective.
May this book serve as a tool to further empower you in your
noble profession. May it inspire you to continue innovating,
learning, and leading in the ever-evolving landscape of
healthcare technology.

Thank you for all that you do, every day.

Contents

Foreword

The field of informatics has evolved significantly over the years, shaping the way healthcare is delivered and managed. One of the most influential groups in the development and expansion of the field has been nurses. While the American Nurses Association (ANA) began acknowledging the significance of nursing informatics in the early 1990s, nurses have always been at the heart of shaping and guiding the use of data and information to improve patient care.

In the mid-19th century, Florence Nightingale's work during the Crimean War laid the foundation for the use of data in healthcare. Faced with appalling sanitary conditions and high mortality rates among soldiers, Nightingale meticulously collected and analyzed data to identify the causes of illness and death. Her innovative use of statistical graphics allowed her to effectively communicate her findings and advocate for sanitary reforms. This early application of data-driven decision-making not only saved countless lives but also underscored the importance of evidence-based practices in nursing.

Informatics as a discipline began to take shape in the mid-20th century with the advent of computers and the realization that these machines could store vast amounts of information and perform complex data processes. The creation of the first Electronic Health Records (EHRs) was initially driven by a vision of automating coding and business processes. When the healthcare industry began bringing EHRs into the clinical realm nurses stepped up with their extensive experience and intimate understanding of clinical workflows to guide its introduction and use on the frontlines of patient care (and yes, we are still working at improving EHRs and the clinician's experience).

Today, the new frontier for nursing informatics is the application of artificial intelligence (AI) and the exponential growth of health and medical data. In the time it takes to read this sentence, thirty percent of all new data created on this planet was health or medically related.

Just as in the past, nurses are uniquely qualified and are critical in guiding and shaping the implementation and use of AI in health and medical practices. Their understanding of clinical workflows allows them to identify areas where AI can streamline processes, reduce workloads, and improve patient outcomes.

And while the use of AI holds great promise in making healthcare better, it also raises significant ethical questions, including issues of privacy, bias, and decision-making. Once again, nurses, as advocates for patients, will play a key role in addressing these concerns. They are among the most qualified clinicians to ensure that AI applications adhere to ethical standards and protect patient privacy.

Beyond improving the delivery of health services, the use of AI and informatics serve another important purpose which is to help "heal the healers."

A benefit of fighting a global pandemic was to shine a light on the nursing workforce crisis. We often talk about this challenge in polite, professional terms. But the reality is this: The systems in which nurses practice which have a mission of healing are harming the very people who are in short supply that are there to take care of the rest of us.

This was the case when we went into the COVID crisis. It remains an issue as I write this foreword today

The integration of artificial intelligence (AI) and machine learning into healthcare has opened new avenues for predictive analytics and personalized medicine. Nurses, equipped with informatics tools, can now identify patterns in patient data, predict potential health issues, and tailor interventions to individual needs, thereby improving patient outcomes and optimizing resource utilization.

In leading such efforts, nurse informaticists can help reduce the cognitive burdens faced by nurses which in turn impacts patient safety and quality of care.

And with some studies showing that up to half of a nurse's time is spent doing things other than direct patient care, such efforts can also lead to a reduction in the number of lower value, repetitive activities nurses being completed by nurses.

This new book by Kathleen McGrow, DNP, MS, RN, PMP, FHIMSS, FAAN provides a comprehensive overview of nursing informatics, highlighting both its historical roots and contemporary applications. It includes case studies, theoretical frameworks, and practical examples that help equip current and future nurses with the knowledge and skills necessary to navigate the complexities of healthcare technology.

Nursing informatics will continue to be at the forefront of healthcare innovation, driving improvements in patient care, operational efficiency, and overall health system performance.

If you are reading this as a nurse, thank you for your skills and commitment to working within today's health system. Harnessing the power of information to advance the nursing profession and enhance the quality of care for all is critical to creating a better system for caregivers and health consumers alike.

Tom Lawry
Author of Hacking Healthcare

Preface

In the ever-changing landscape of healthcare, I've observed how technology has become a game-changer. It holds the promise to revolutionize patient care, streamline processes, and enhance health outcomes. However, the key to unlocking this potential, I believe, lies with those who are at the heart of patient care—our nurses.

Empowering Nurses with Technology: A Practical Guide to Nurse Informatics is my attempt to guide nurses venturing into the field of informatics. This book is designed to bridge the gap between the art of nursing and the science of technology, offering practical insights into how technology can be harnessed to enhance the nursing profession.

The book is structured into ten chapters, each focusing on a different facet of nurse informatics. It starts with the basics of healthcare technology, introducing nurses to the digital tools and systems prevalent in today's healthcare landscape. As the book progresses, it delves deeper into the world of informatics, exploring advanced concepts and technologies that are shaping the future of healthcare.

But this book is not just about understanding technology; it's also about empowering nurses to use technology to improve patient care. It's about showing nurses that they are not only passive users of technology, but also active participants in the digital transformation of healthcare.

They can be innovators, leaders, and change-makers, using technology to enhance patient care and improve health outcomes.

Whether you're a nursing student just starting your journey, a seasoned nurse looking to update your tech skills, or a nurse informaticist aiming to deepen your knowledge, this book is for you. It's a practical, hands-on guide that will empower you to take an active role in shaping the future of healthcare.

I invite you to embark on this journey with me. I hope that this book will serve as a valuable resource in your professional development, contributing to your growth as a nurse and nurse informaticist, and, ultimately, to the betterment of patient care. Thank you for choosing to read this book. I look forward to empowering you with the knowledge and skills to navigate the exciting intersection of nursing and technology.

Kathleen McGrow

Acknowledgments

Writing *Empowering Nurses with Technology: A Practical Guide to Nurse Informatics* has been a journey of discovery and growth for me. This book, a testament to my passion and commitment, could not have come to fruition without the support and guidance of many.

I wish to express my heartfelt gratitude and appreciation to those who have supported this endeavor.

- Tom Lawry
- Dr. Marisa Wilson DNSc, MHSc, RN-BC, CPHIMS, FAMIA, FIAHSI, FAAN (in memory)

Their wisdom, insights, and patience have been invaluable in shaping this guide. Their shared belief in the transformative power of technology for nurses has been a beacon that guided my work.

About the Author

 **Kathleen McGrow**, who holds a Doctor of Nursing Practice degree from the University of Maryland, Baltimore, serves as the Global Chief Nursing Information Officer at Microsoft. In her role, she guides organizations on how to apply innovative technologies to enhance clinical performance, patient experience, and transform care models. She is skilled in leveraging technology to address digital transformation needs, including workforce crisis, consumer and patient engagement, and cognitive computing for a learning health system.

With a wealth of clinical experience in trauma critical care, McGrow is an internationally recognized authority in the intersection of clinical care and technology. She has delivered numerous educational presentations to professional groups, including the International Congress of Nursing in Montreal, Canada.

In addition to her role at Microsoft, McGrow co-chairs the HIMSS Nursing Innovation Advisory Committee and serves as an adjunct clinical instructor at University of Alabama, School of Nursing. Her work continues to inspire and guide the nursing community in the digital age.

Introduction

Welcome to *Empowering Nurses with Technology: A Practical Guide to Nurse Informatics*. I am thrilled to have you join me on this journey of discovery and empowerment. My journey into the world of nursing informatics began in the bustling corridors of The Shock Trauma Center in Baltimore, Maryland, where I worked as a bedside nurse in the Trauma Resuscitation Unit (TRU). One day, an 18-year-old female car driver was brought in post a motor vehicle crash with a roll over. Her left arm had flown out of the window, crushing her hand. She was going to the operating room for wound wash out, complete amputation of left thumb, and hand salvage procedure. Time was of the essence, and I found myself at the computer terminal at the nurses' station, searching for her lab results, as she had significant blood loss.

At the time (1997), nurses had limited access to information via the computer, mainly admission demographics and laboratory results. There was no computer mouse, so I typed in the string command of "2.3.1" for hematology results and then "2.3.2" for chemistry results. The lab values seemed to take forever to load, and I asked my coworker, "Why can't I see all the labs on the screen at the same time"? Her reply, "Because some engineers in the basement built this shi*t and they never asked us what we wanted". This statement, casual as it was, sparked a lot of questions for me. Who were these engineers? Why did they not talk to us, the nurses, and learn what we needed and wanted? Why were they in the basement?

These questions started many thought processes. As I continued working in the TRU, I saw the increasing use of computers and technology for patient care. I came to believe that as nurses, we need to make an impact on the information systems in which we work. Nurses need to own our workflows. Nurses should communicate our needs for the information systems we are using. Nurses should collaborate with and direct the developers and programmers that work on the information systems we use. It is our professional responsibility to ensure we have input, to make healthcare better for both clinicians and our patients.

That's why I wrote this book – to empower nurses like you to bridge this gap. This book is more than just a guide; it's a journey into the world of nursing informatics. It's about understanding the potential of technology in nursing and learning how to use it effectively. It's about becoming not just a user of technology, but an innovator and a leader in the digital transformation of healthcare.

In the following chapters, we will explore the basics of healthcare technology, delve into advanced informatics concepts, and learn how to apply these concepts in real-world nursing scenarios. We will explore practical examples and actionable advice to help you navigate the digital landscape of healthcare.

But more than anything, this book is about empowerment. It's about empowering you, the nurse, to take an active role in shaping the future of healthcare. It's about showing you that you are not just a passive user of technology, but a key player in the digital transformation of healthcare.

I invite you to join me on this journey. Let's explore the fascinating nexus of nursing and technology together.

Chapter 1

Basics of Nursing Informatics

Introduction

Nursing informatics is a discipline that developed in the 1960s when the healthcare industry started to use computer technology for clinical and administrative purposes. The American Nurses Association (ANA) acknowledged the significance of nursing informatics in the early 1990s and described it as "a blend of computer science, information science, and nursing science that helps with the management and processing of nursing data, information, and knowledge to support the practice of nursing and the delivery of patient care".[1]

Nursing informatics has evolved over the years, adapting to advances in technology and changes in healthcare delivery models. The field has expanded to encompass a wide range of activities, including the development of electronic health records (EHRs), clinical decision support systems (CDSSs), telehealth, and patient monitoring systems. Nursing informatics aims to improve the quality, safety, efficiency, and effectiveness of healthcare by using information and communication technologies to support decision-making, coordination, and collaboration among healthcare professionals and patients.

Nursing informatics also involves the development, implementation, and evaluation of information systems, standards, policies, and ethical issues related to nursing practice and education. Nursing informatics is an interdisciplinary field that draws from various domains, such as nursing, computer science, information science, cognitive science, human factors, organizational science, and health policy. Nursing informatics is recognized as a specialty by the ANA and has its own certification, competencies, scope, and standards of practice. Nursing informatics is a dynamic and evolving field that responds to the changing needs and challenges of the healthcare environment.

The importance of nursing informatics in healthcare cannot be overstated. With the mounting complexity of healthcare delivery and the growing volume of patient data, the use of technology and information science has become essential for managing patient care. Nursing informatics facilitates the efficient and accurate communication of patient information among healthcare providers, improving care coordination and patient safety. It also enables healthcare providers to make evidence-based decisions and interventions, leading to improved patient outcomes.

Nursing informatics has also contributed to the development of patient-centered care. By giving patients access to their health records and empowering them to participate in their care, nursing informatics promotes patient engagement and self-management. Patients can communicate with healthcare providers through portals and telehealth platforms, monitor their health status, and receive personalized health education. These contributions were taken into consideration for the development of the updated definition: "Nursing informatics is the specialty that transforms data into needed information and leverages technologies to improve health and healthcare equity, safety, quality, and outcomes".[2]

Nursing informatics is a vital component of modern healthcare, integrating technology and information science to improve patient outcomes and enhance the quality of care provided.

Nursing informatics professionals use various tools and methods to collect, manage, analyze, and communicate health data to support clinical decision-making and improve patient outcomes. As the healthcare system becomes more complex and dynamic, nursing informatics will remain an essential component of promoting patient-centered, evidence-based, and cost-effective care.

Definition of Nursing Informatics

Nursing informatics is defined as the use of information technology, data science, and healthcare information systems to manage and communicate patient data. It is a subfield of nursing that involves the application of technology and information science to enhance the quality and effectiveness of patient care delivery. Nursing informatics integrates the principles of nursing science, computer science, and information science to support patient-centered care, clinical decision-making, and research.

Nursing informatics emerged in the 1960s when hospitals began using computer technology to manage patient data.

However, it was not until the 1990s that nursing informatics began to gain recognition as a specialized field of nursing. In 1992, the ANA recognized nursing informatics as a nursing specialty.[3] Since then, nursing informatics has evolved to become an integral part of healthcare, playing a crucial role in improving patient outcomes and enhancing the quality of care provided.

The field of nursing informatics has continued to evolve since its inception. In the early years, nursing informatics focused mainly on automating patient data management, such as scheduling appointments and managing medical records. However, with the advent of EHRs, nursing informatics has become more focused on utilizing data to support clinical decision-making and patient-centered care.

As healthcare technology has continued to advance, nursing informatics has become increasingly important in healthcare delivery. With the widespread adoption of EHRs, nurse informaticists are now responsible for managing, analyzing, and interpreting large amounts of patient data to help improve patient outcomes. This includes utilizing data analytics and machine learning algorithms to identify patterns and trends in patient data, which can help healthcare providers make more informed decisions about patient care.

Nursing informatics is essential not only for patient care but also for healthcare research. Nurse informaticists can use data from EHRs and other healthcare information systems to help identify areas for improvement in healthcare delivery and outcomes, as well as potential research questions and areas of inquiry. For example, nurse informaticists can use data analytics to evaluate the effectiveness of different interventions, such as medication adherence, self-management, or telehealth, on patient outcomes. They can also use data mining to discover new knowledge and insights from large and complex datasets, such as identifying risk factors, predicting outcomes, or finding associations among variables. Furthermore, nurse informaticists can use data visualization to present and communicate their findings in a clear and engaging way, such as using graphs, charts, maps, or dashboards. By utilizing data from various sources, nurse informaticists can contribute to the advancement of healthcare research and evidence-based practice.

As stated, the goal of nursing informatics is to improve the quality of healthcare and patient outcomes using technology and data. The data, information, knowledge, and wisdom (DIKW) framework is a theoretical model that illustrates the relationships between data, information, knowledge, and wisdom.[4] In nursing informatics, the DIKW framework is often used to guide the development and implementation of technology solutions in healthcare.

> According to the DIKW framework, data refers to raw facts and figures that have not been organized or analyzed. Information is data that has been processed and organized in a meaningful way. Knowledge is information that has been analyzed, synthesized, and understood in the context of a particular situation. Wisdom is the ability to apply knowledge in a way that results in wise decision-making.[5]

The DIKW framework can guide the creation of technology solutions that help healthcare providers handle data in ways that produce useful information and knowledge to enhance patient outcomes. For instance, EHRs can gather and keep patient data, which can be examined to produce findings that can improve patient care. Likewise, CDSS can offer healthcare providers timely, evidence-based suggestions to help them make smart decisions about patient care (Figure 1.1).

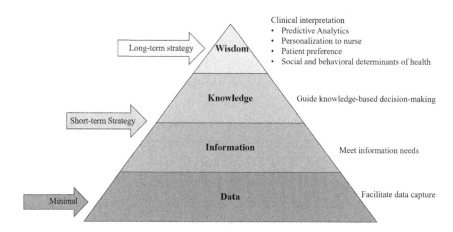

Figure 1.1   DIKW strategic plan. (Reproduced from Cato KD, McGrow K, Rossetti SC. Transforming clinical data into wisdom: artificial intelligence implications for nurse leaders. Nurs Manage. 2020;51(11):24–30. doi: 10.1097/01. NUMA.0000719396.83518.d6. PMID: 33086364; PMCID: PMC8018525.)

Overall, nursing informatics has become an integral part of modern healthcare delivery. As technology continues to advance and healthcare becomes increasingly data-driven, nurse informaticists will continue to play a crucial role in improving patient outcomes and enhancing the quality of care provided.

Common Frameworks and Models Used in Nursing Informatics

Nursing Process Model (NPM)

The nursing process model (NPM) is a fundamental framework in nursing practice, encompassing five key steps: assessment, diagnosis, planning, implementation, and evaluation.[6] The nursing process begins with an assessment, which is the first step where nurses gather comprehensive information about the patient's physical, psychological, sociocultural, and spiritual status. This data collection is crucial as it forms the basis of the care plan. Based on the assessment, the next step is diagnosis, where nurses identify the patient's health issues, risks, and needs. These are often formulated as nursing diagnoses, which guide the next steps of planning and implementation. In the planning stage, nurses develop a detailed care plan tailored to the patient's needs. This includes setting measurable and achievable short- and long-term goals and deciding on the nursing actions to achieve these goals. Following planning, the care plan is put into action during the implementation stage. Nursing interventions are performed to meet the goals set in the planning stage. These interventions could be preventive, therapeutic, or health-promotion activities. The final step of the nursing process is evaluation. This involves evaluating the effectiveness of nursing care by comparing the patient's health outcomes with the set goals. Based on this evaluation, the care plan may be continued, modified, or terminated.

Much of the collected assessment data is entered into the EHR to have a comprehensive view of the patient's condition. The integration of information technology into NPM can greatly enhance clinical decision-making and patient-care processes. For instance, the EHR can streamline the assessment process by providing easy access to patient data. Decision support systems can assist in the diagnosis and planning stages by providing evidence-based recommendations. During the implementation stage, information technology can aid in monitoring patient's health status and administering treatments. Finally, data analytics tools can support the evaluation of patient outcomes and the effectiveness of the care provided. It is important to note that while technology can support and enhance nursing practice, it does not replace the critical thinking, clinical judgment, and compassionate care provided by nurses. The NPM serves as a reminder of the holistic and patient-centered nature of nursing care.[7]

Nurses' familiarity with the NPM framework equips them with the ability to adapt and adopt the nursing informatics frameworks and models. This is particularly useful when deploying the information technology utilized in their practice. Furthermore, nurse informaticists have a solid foundation for utilizing and implementing information technology frameworks and models.

Health information and technology frameworks and models are essential tools for understanding how technology and data can be used to improve patient care and healthcare outcomes. They provide a structure for organizing and interpreting data, as well as a framework for understanding how technology can be used to support clinical decision-making and patient-care processes.

Technology Acceptance Model (TAM)

The technology acceptance model (TAM), a popular framework, concentrates on user attitudes and behaviors towards technology. It proposes that user acceptance and adoption are significantly influenced by the perceived usefulness and ease of use of technology. This model is grounded in the psychological theory of reasoned action and the theory of planned behavior. It assumes that two variables, perceived ease of use and perceived usefulness, play a mediating role in the intricate relationship between the system and user acceptance.[8]

■ Perceived usefulness: This is defined as the extent to which a user is convinced that utilizing a specific system would boost their work performance.[8]

■ Perceived ease of use: This is the extent to which a user thinks that the use of a specific system would require minimal effort.[8]

The TAM has been widely used to understand the acceptance of various technologies. For instance, it has been used to explore healthcare providers' and administrators' perceptions of the usefulness and ease of using technology in palliative care.[9]

Unified Theory of Acceptance and Use of Technology (UTAUT)

The unified theory of acceptance and use of technology (UTAUT) is an extension of TAM and includes additional factors that influence user acceptance and adoption of technology.[10]

The UTAUT model presents four primary constructs:

1. Performance expectancy: It refers to the extent to which a person is convinced that utilizing the system will enhance their work efficiency.
2. Effort expectancy: It signifies the level of comfort linked with employing the system.
3. Social influence: It represents how much a person perceives that others believe they should use the new system.
4. Facilitating conditions: Indicates how strongly a person is persuaded that organizational and technical support is available for using the system.

In addition to these, the UTAUT model also considers variables such as gender, age, experience, and voluntariness of use.[10]

Clinical Decision Support System (CDSS)

The clinical decision support system (CDSS) model focuses on the use of technology to support clinical decision-making.[11] It includes the development of algorithms and rules that can assist in clinical decision-making, including patient data analysis to provide healthcare providers with recommendations for diagnosis, treatment, and monitoring. Patient-specific assessments and recommendations assist healthcare providers in improving patient care and healthcare delivery.

CDSS has two types of models: knowledge-based and non-knowledge-based systems.

Knowledge-based systems: These systems are equipped with a knowledgebase and utilize a set of rules to process existing data, leading to a solution. The rules are typically structured as if–then statements and are formulated based on evidence from literature, practices, or patients.[12] The system pulls data for the evaluation of these rules and generates an action or output accordingly.

Non-knowledge-based systems: In contrast, these systems employ machine learning to scrutinize clinical data. They learn by observing patterns in basic task execution and from examples. The decision-making process is driven by artificial intelligence (AI), machine learning (ML), or statistical pattern recognition rather than relying on pre-programmed expert medical knowledge.[12] Despite the rapidly growing use of the application of AI in medicine, non-knowledge-based CDSS face numerous challenges, including difficulties in comprehending the logic behind AI recommendations (often referred to as "black boxes") and issues related to data availability.

These systems can significantly enhance clinical performance by reducing medical errors, improving patient safety, and increasing patient outcomes.[13] Key components of a CDSS include a dynamic medical knowledgebase and a mechanism to match patient-specific data with the knowledgebase. A well-designed CDSS can also incorporate patient data from EHRs, genetic information, and relevant clinical research.

Human Factors Engineering (HFE)

The human factors engineering (HFE) model focuses on the interaction between technology, end-users, and the environment. It includes the design and evaluation of technology to ensure that it is user-friendly, efficient, and safe. HFE in healthcare, also known as healthcare ergonomics or usability engineering, is the application of knowledge about human capabilities and limitations to the design and development of healthcare systems and equipment. HFE utilizes knowledge about human behavior, skills, constraints, and other traits in the creation of tools, machinery, systems, tasks, occupations, and environments to ensure productive, secure, comfortable, and efficient use by humans.[14]

HFE in healthcare is a multidisciplinary field that involves many disciplines, such as psychology, sociology, biomedical engineering, biomechanics, industrial design, physiology, anthropometry, interaction design, visual design, user experience, and user interface design. It aims to reduce human error, increase productivity, and enhance patient safety and comfort with a specific focus on the interaction between healthcare professionals and medical devices or systems.[15]

The HFE model in healthcare focuses on the interaction between medical technology, healthcare professionals, and the clinical environment and uses a systemic approach. It includes the design and evaluation of medical technology to ensure that it is user-friendly, efficient, and safe. This involves a wide range of major design considerations, including but not limited to ergonomics, anatomy, demographics, psychology, organizational dynamics, the effects of physical environments on the healthcare professional, human reliability, and human information processing.[15]

The development of any healthcare system's concept of operations is highly dependent on the role of the healthcare professional in the capabilities and operation of the system. HFE in healthcare includes task analysis, workload analysis, task allocation (between humans, teams, automation, and systems), human performance analysis, human error analysis, anthropometric analysis (the size of humans as it relates to their tasks, environment, and tools), display design, and control design. Human factors engineers adopt a systematic strategy to ensure that a system is designed to cater to human needs rather than requiring humans to adjust to the system. This approach enables humans to perform optimally, make the most informed decisions, reduce both physical and mental strain, and derive personal satisfaction.[14]

HFE should be a part of the design of healthcare systems from the beginning of the acquisition process. Healthcare professionals are the most important part of any healthcare system, and the capabilities of the healthcare professional in systems should be part of the lifecycle of the process and the project. HFE is an essential aspect of the healthcare design process that ensures the medical system or equipment design, required human tasks, and clinical work environment are compatible with the sensory, perceptual, mental, and physical attributes of the healthcare personnel who will operate, maintain, control, and support it.[15]

Socio-technical Systems (STSs) Model

Socio-technical systems (STSs) model represents a design philosophy that considers human, social, organizational, and technical aspects in the creation of organizational systems. With a rich history, STSs model aims to ensure a holistic consideration of both technical and organizational elements of a system.[16] The fundamental belief of socio-technical thinking is that the design of systems should be a process that incorporates both social and technical factors influencing the functionality and utilization of computer-based systems. In the realm of health information technology (HIT), STSs model assumes a pivotal role. A novel socio-technical model has been formulated to examine HIT within complex adaptive healthcare systems. This model presents an eight-dimensional framework explicitly crafted to tackle the socio-technical challenges associated with the design, development, implementation, usage, and evaluation of HIT. These eight dimensions are not independent, sequential, or hierarchical but are interdependent and interconnected concepts akin to other complex adaptive systems' compositions.[17] According to Sittig and Singh, the eight dimensions encompass:

■ Hardware and software computing infrastructure
■ Clinical content
■ The human–computer interface
■ People
■ Workflow and communication

- Internal organizational features (e.g., environment, policies, procedures, and culture)
- External rules and regulations
- Measurement and monitoring

These dimensions aid in comprehending how human, social, and organizational factors influence work methods and the usage of technical systems. This understanding can inform the design of organizational structures, business processes, and technical systems.

In brief, these frameworks and models can be used in various practical applications in healthcare. For example, the CDSS model can be used to develop and implement decision support systems that improve clinical decision-making and patient outcomes. The NPM model can be used to develop and implement EHRs that support the nursing process and improve patient-care processes. The HFE model can be used to design and evaluate the usability and safety of medical devices and other technology used in healthcare. Table 1.1 provides an overview of various frameworks and models used in nursing informatics. Each model is discussed in terms of its application in healthcare, focusing on improving patient care and healthcare outcomes.

Frameworks and models provide the nurse informaticist with a structure for understanding how technology and data can be used to improve patient care and healthcare outcomes. They can be used in various practical applications in healthcare, such as the development of decision support systems, EHRs, and medical devices. Understanding and applying these frameworks and models are essential for nursing informatics professionals to succeed in their roles as thought leaders in healthcare.

Table 1.1   Common Frameworks and Models Used in Nursing Informatics

Framework/Model	Definition
Nursing process model (NPM)[7]	The NPM is a widely used framework for nursing practice that includes assessment, diagnosis, planning, implementation, and evaluation. The use of technology can be integrated into each of these steps to support clinical decision-making and patient-care processes.
Technology acceptance model (TAM)[8]	The TAM is a widely used framework that focuses on the attitudes and behaviors of users towards technology. It suggests that the perceived usefulness and ease of use of technology are significant determinants of user acceptance and adoption.
Unified theory of acceptance and use of technology (UTAUT)[10]	The UTAUT model is an extension of the TAM model and incorporates additional factors that influence user acceptance and adoption of technology. These include social influence, facilitating conditions, and behavioral intention.
Clinical decision support system (CDSS)[11]	The CDSS model focuses on the use of technology to support clinical decision-making. It includes the development of algorithms and rules that can analyze patient data and provide clinicians with recommendations for diagnosis, treatment, and monitoring.
Human factors engineering (HFE)[14]	The HFE model focuses on the interaction between technology, users, and the environment. It includes the design and evaluation of technology to ensure that it is user-friendly, efficient, and safe.
Socio-technical systems (STSs)[16]	The STSs model represents a design philosophy that takes into account human, social, organizational, and technical aspects in the creation of organizational system.

Importance of Nursing Informatics in Healthcare

Nursing informatics is vital in healthcare because it allows healthcare providers to gather, manage, and examine patient data, offering them useful information for patient care. Nursing informatics has a crucial role in healthcare by giving healthcare providers a complete picture of patient data. Using sophisticated healthcare information systems, nurse informaticists can gather and examine patient data from different sources, such as laboratory tests, medical images, and other healthcare records. By examining this data, healthcare providers can check patient health status, detect possible health problems, track patient improvement, and create customized care plans to suit individual patient needs.

One of the benefits of nursing informatics is that it enhances patient safety by reducing the risk of potential errors in medication administration and patient data management. By utilizing EHRs and computerized provider order entry (CPOE) systems, healthcare providers can access patient data quickly and make informed decisions about patient care. These systems also reduce the risk of miscommunication, duplication, and omission of information that can lead to adverse events.

Furthermore, nursing informatics supports evidence-based practice by providing healthcare providers with access to current research and clinical practice guidelines. This enables healthcare providers to make informed decisions about patient care based on the best available evidence. Evidence-based practice also improves the quality and outcomes of patient care, as well as the efficiency and cost-effectiveness of healthcare delivery.

Nursing informatics supports effective communication and enhances collaboration among healthcare providers.

By utilizing electronic health records, healthcare providers can access patient data quickly and easily, providing a more streamlined and seamless delivery of care. This enables healthcare providers to work together more effectively and communicate more efficiently, ensuring that patients receive timely and appropriate care.

Another role of nursing informatics is to manage information technology systems that may minimize the risk of errors in medication administration and patient data management. By utilizing CPOE systems, healthcare providers can enter medication orders directly into an electronic health record, reducing the risk of transcription errors and ensuring patients receive the correct medication and dosage. Nursing informatics plays a key role in ensuring the accuracy and completeness of patient data, reducing the risk of errors in patient care.

Furthermore, nursing informatics supports evidence-based practice by providing healthcare providers with access to up-to-date research and clinical practice guidelines. This enables healthcare providers to make informed decisions about patient care based on the best available evidence, improving patient outcomes and enhancing the quality of care provided. By utilizing nursing informatics, healthcare providers can ensure they are delivering care based on the latest evidence and best practices, which helps to improve patient safety and overall healthcare quality.

In conclusion, nursing informatics is essential in healthcare delivery as it enables nurses and other healthcare providers to collect, manage, and analyze patient data, providing them with valuable insights into patient care. It supports effective communication and collaboration among healthcare providers, reduces the risk of errors in medication administration and patient data management, and supports evidence-based practice. As healthcare becomes increasingly data-driven, nursing informatics will continue to play an increasingly important role in healthcare delivery, improving patient outcomes and enhancing the quality of care provided.

Improving Patient Outcomes with Nursing Informatics

Nursing informatics is a vital part of healthcare delivery that influences patient outcomes. Nursing informatics improves patient outcomes by enabling efficient patient care delivery. By using data analytics and decision support systems, healthcare providers can collect and examine patient data to create customized care plans based on individual patient needs. This helps to ensure patients get the appropriate care at the right time and in the right place, which can lead to better patient outcomes.

One of the key benefits of nursing informatics is its ability to support patient education and engagement. Through patient portals, patients can access their health information, including medical records, test results, and other health-related information. This not only helps patients to be more informed about their health, but it also empowers them to take an active role in their care, which can lead to better health outcomes.

In addition, nursing informatics can help improve medication management and reduce medication errors. Utilization of CPOE and bar-code medication administration (BCMA) technology ensures medications are accurately entered into the patient record and safely administered, reducing the risk of errors in medication administration errors.[18] Another important benefit of nursing informatics is its ability to support evidence-based practice.

Moreover, nursing informatics can also enhance patient safety by enabling the exchange of patient data and fostering communication among healthcare providers. This helps to ensure patient information is exchanged accurately and effectively, reducing the risk of errors and improving the quality of care delivered.

Nursing informatics is essential for enhancing and improving patient outcomes by enabling efficient patient care delivery, promoting patient education and engagement, streamlining medication management, fostering evidence-based practice, and improving patient safety. As technology advances, nursing informatics will continue to play a growing role in healthcare delivery, supporting better patient outcomes and enhancing the quality of care provided.

In summary, nursing informatics is a specialized field of nursing that integrates technology and information science to manage and communicate patient data. The evolution of nursing informatics has transformed the way patient care is delivered, improving patient outcomes and enhancing the quality of care provided. Nursing informatics is essential in healthcare as it enables healthcare providers to collect, manage, and analyze patient data, providing valuable insights into patient care. By utilizing nursing informatics, healthcare providers can monitor patient health status, identify potential health risks, and develop personalized care plans to meet individual patient needs, resulting in better health outcomes for patients.

References

1. Sweeney J. Healthcare informatics. Online J Nurs Informat. 2017;21(1).
2. American Nurses Association. *Nursing Informatics: Scope and Standards of Practice*. 3rd ed. Silver Spring, MD: American Nurses Association, 2022.

3. Bickford CJ. The professional association's perspective on nursing informatics and competencies in the US. Stud Health Technol Inform. 2017;232:62–68. PMID: 28106583.

4. Graves JR, Corcoran S. The study of nursing informatics. Image J Knurs Sch. 1989;21(4):227–231.

5. Targowski A. From data to wisdom. Dialog Universal. 2005;15(5):55–71.

6. Glasper A. *Strategies to ensure that all patients have a personalised nursing care plan*, n.d. Retrieved December 20, 2023, from www.britishjournalofnursing.com/content/healthc are-policy/strategies-to-ensure-that-all-patients-have-a-personali sed-nursing-care-plan.

7. Ajibade B. *Assessing the patient's needs and planning effective care*. n.d. Retrieved December 20, 2023, from www.britishjourn alofnursing.com/content/clinical/assessing-the-patients-needs-and-planning-effective-care.

8. Marangunić N, Granić A. Technology acceptance model: a literature review from 1986 to 2013. Univ Access Inf Soc. 2015;14:81–95. https://doi.org/10.1007/s10209-014-0348-1.

9. Nguyen M, Fujioka J, Wentlandt K, Onabajo, N., Wong, I., Bhatia, R. S., Bhattacharyya, O., & Stamenova, V. Using the technology acceptance model to explore health provider and administrator perceptions of the usefulness and ease of using technology in palliative care. BMC Palliat Care. 2020;19:138. https://doi.org/10.1186/s12904-020-00644-8.

10. Marikyan D, Papagiannidis S. Unified theory of acceptance and use of technology: a review. In S. Papagiannidis (Ed.), *TheoryHub Book*. United Kingdom: TheoryHub, 2023. Available at https://open.ncl.ac.uk /; ISBN: 9781739604400.

11. Zikos D, DeLellis N. CDSS-RM: a clinical decision support system reference model. BMC Med Res Methodol. 2018;18:137. https://doi.org/10.1186/s12874-018-0587-6.

12. Sutton RT, Pincock D, Baumgart DC, Sadowski DC, Fedorak RN, Kroeker KI. An overview of clinical decision support systems: benefits, risks, and strategies for success. NPJ Digit Med. 2020;3(1):1–10. https://doi.org/10.1038/s41 746-020-0221-y>.

13. Hak F, Guimarães T, Santos M. Towards effective clinical decision support systems: a systematic review. PLoS ONE.

2022;17(8):e0272846. https://doi.org/10.1371/journal.
pone.0272846.

14. Vasquez HM, Pianarosa E, Sirbu R, Diemert LM, Cunningham
HV, Donmez B, Rosella LC. Human factors applications in the
design of decision support systems for population health: a
scoping review. BMJ Open. 2022;12(4):1–6. https://doi.org/
10.1136/bmjopen-2021-054330.

15. Ponnala S, Rivera AJ. Human factors engineering: status,
interventions, future directions in pediatrics. Curr Treat
Opt Pediat. 2019;5(2):145–164. https://doi.org/10.1007/s40
746-019-00157-4.

16. Baxter G, Sommerville I. Socio-technical systems: from
design methods to systems engineering. Interact Comput.
2011;23(1):4–17. https://doi.org/10.1016/j.intcom.2010.07.003.

17. Sittig DF, Singh H. A new sociotechnical model for studying
health information technology in complex adaptive healthcare
systems. Qual Saf Health Care. 2010;19(Suppl 3):1–14. https://
doi.org/10.1136/qshc.2010.042085

18. Thompson KM, Swanson KM, Cox DL, Kirchner RB, Russell
JJ, Wermers RA, Storlie CB, Johnson MG, Naessens JM.
Implementation of bar-code medication administration to
reduce patient harm. Mayo Clin Proc Innov Qual Outcomes.
2018;2(4):342–351. doi: 10.1016/j.mayocpiqo.2018.09.001.
PMID: 30560236; PMCID: PMC6257885.

Chapter 2

Electronic Health Records

History and Evolution of EHRs

Electronic health records (EHRs) have a rich history that spans over several decades. The earliest electronic records were developed during the 1960s and 1970s, primarily for administrative purposes such as billing and scheduling. However, it was not until the 1990s that EHRs started to gain prominence in healthcare, with the development of more sophisticated computer systems and the increasing availability of digital data storage.

During the 1980s and early 1990s, the development of more sophisticated computer systems and the increasing availability of digital data storage led to the emergence of EHRs as a tool for healthcare providers. Initially, EHRs were primarily used for collecting patient information and documentation, including progress notes.[1]

However, as technology advanced, EHRs became more integrated into healthcare delivery, with the ability to store

 DOI: 10.4324/9781003439721-2

and analyze more significant amounts of patient data. In the mid-1990s, the Institute of Medicine (IOM) recognized the potential benefits of EHRs and called for their widespread adoption in healthcare.[2] This led to increased government funding for the development, implementation, and deployment of EHRs and the establishment of standards for their use and interoperability.

During the 2000s, the adoption of EHRs began to accelerate with the development of more user-friendly and interoperable systems. The passage of the Health Information Technology for Economic and Clinical Health (HITECH) act in 2009 provided financial incentives for healthcare providers to adopt and use EHRs, further driving their adoption.[3] Capabilities such as clinical decision support systems (CDSSs), computerized provider order entry (CPOE), and health information exchange (HIE) are seen as key to improving healthcare quality and cost reductions.[4]

Today, EHRs have become an essential tool in healthcare delivery. They provide healthcare providers with quick and easy access to patient data and support better clinical decision-making. They also enable improved communication and collaboration among healthcare providers and provide a platform for data analysis and research.

EHRs have a rich history that spans several decades, with their development and adoption driven by advancements in technology, government initiatives, and the need for more efficient and effective healthcare delivery. As technology evolves, EHRs will continue to play an increasingly important role in healthcare, supporting better patient outcomes and enhancing the quality of care provided. This aligns with the Quintuple Aim, which is focused on better health, improved patient outcomes, clinician wellbeing, and health equity.[5]

The Quintuple Aim is a comprehensive framework that underscores the pressing need for health systems to prioritize health equity, along with cost-efficiency, population health, patient experience, and the wellbeing of healthcare providers.[6]

The Quintuple Aim emphasizes health equity, which ensures that everyone, regardless of socioeconomic status, race, ethnicity, or other characteristics, has a fair and just opportunity to be as healthy as possible.[7]

Cost-efficiency refers to the reduction of healthcare costs per person. It involves implementing strategies that provide high-quality care at lower costs. Population health involves improving the health outcomes of a group of individuals, including the distribution of such outcomes within the group. Patient experience includes several aspects of healthcare delivery that patients value, such as timely appointments, easy access to information, and good communication with healthcare providers. Addressing clinician burnout is a critical aspect of the Quintuple Aim. It recognizes the importance of the healthcare workforce's wellbeing in achieving the primary goal of improving population health.[8]

The Quintuple Aim encourages health systems to view all decisions through the lens of these five aims simultaneously. It acknowledges that improving health and reducing costs at the expense of clinician wellbeing impedes progress overall. Therefore, health systems must balance these five aims to optimize health system performance. The Quintuple Aim reflects the urgency for health systems to address health equity in addition to cost, population health, patient experience, and employee wellbeing goals (Figure 2.1).[5]

EHRs are instrumental in fulfilling the objectives of the Quintuple Aim in healthcare. They allow medical professionals to exchange precise and current patient

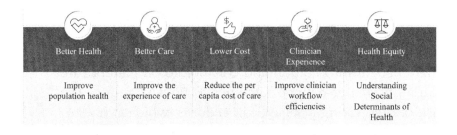

Better Health	Better Care	Lower Cost	Clinician Experience	Health Equity
Improve population health	Improve the experience of care	Reduce the per capita cost of care	Improve clinician workflow efficiencies	Understanding Social Determinants of Health

Figure 2.1 Quintuple Aim. (Modified from Itchhaporia D. The evolution of the quintuple aim: health equity, health outcomes, and the economy. J Am Coll Cardiol. 2021;78(22):2262–2264. doi: 10.1016/ j.jacc.2021.10.018. PMID: 34823665; PMCID: PMC8608191.)

data, enhancing care coordination and improving patient experience, a vital goal of the Quintuple Aim. EHRs also aid in minimizing the expensive repetition of tests and procedures, thereby reducing healthcare costs, another aim of the Quintuple Aim. By offering a detailed view of a patient's health history, EHRs facilitate informed decision-making, leading to better population health. Furthermore, EHRs promote health equity, the fifth aim of the Quintuple Aim, by guaranteeing that all patients, irrespective of their socioeconomic status, have equal access to their health information. Lastly, by simplifying administrative tasks and enhancing the efficiency of care delivery, EHRs also help improve the wellbeing of clinicians.

Benefits of Using EHRs

The use of EHRs has several advantages in healthcare, including improving the quality and safety of patient care, increasing the efficiency and productivity of healthcare providers, and reducing healthcare costs. EHRs allow for better communication and coordination among healthcare providers, resulting in better patient outcomes and reduced medical errors. With EHRs, healthcare providers can easily share patient information and collaborate on patient care, leading to better patient outcomes. EHRs also reduce the risk of duplicating tests and procedures, which can lead to significant cost savings for patients and healthcare organizations. They also provide a more comprehensive view of a patient's medical history, allowing healthcare providers to make more informed decisions.

EHRs provide a centralized location for storing and accessing patient information, including medical history, lab results, and medication records. This allows healthcare providers to make more informed decisions about patient care.

EHRs are a vital tool in modern healthcare, offering numerous benefits that enhance patient safety. They provide healthcare providers access to complete and up-to-date patient data, which aids in making informed decisions, ensuring the proper treatment and minimizing adverse events. One of the significant advantages of EHRs is their ability to reduce the risk of medical errors, such as prescribing the wrong medication or administering the wrong dose. EHRs can expose potential safety problems when they occur, helping healthcare providers avoid more severe consequences for patients and leading to better patient outcomes.

In addition, EHRs allow for real-time monitoring and tracking of patient vital signs. This feature makes detecting potential health risks easier and intervening before a medical crisis occurs. EHRs also play a transformative role in healthcare by improving medication safety, making patient health information available at the point of care, and facilitating care coordination. By streamlining administrative tasks and improving the efficiency of care delivery, EHRs can also contribute to enhancing the healthcare system's overall efficiency.

EHRs provide a more efficient and productive way to manage patient care. They eliminate the need for paper records, reducing the time and effort required for record-keeping and documentation. EHRs also streamline administrative processes, such as billing and insurance claims, resulting in faster reimbursements and reduced paperwork.

EHRs serve as a vital resource in modern healthcare, offering comprehensive data that can be utilized for a broad spectrum of research purposes. This includes clinical research, health services research, and epidemiological studies. In clinical research, EHRs significantly enhance the process by providing patient data, including medical history, diagnoses, medications, treatment plans, immunization dates, allergies, radiology images, and laboratory and test results. This information aids in studying the effectiveness of various treatments, understanding disease progression, and developing new therapeutic strategies.

In health services research, EHRs examine how people access healthcare, the costs associated with care, and patient outcomes resulting from this care. The data in EHRs provides valuable insights into patterns of care, health outcomes, and cost-effectiveness.

For epidemiological studies, EHRs are a valuable resource that seek to understand the patterns, causes, and effects of health and disease conditions in defined populations. The vast amount of data in EHRs allows researchers to study disease trends and patterns on a population level, leading to better disease prevention and control strategies.

Furthermore, researchers can analyze the data in EHRs to identify patterns and trends in patient health. These analyses can provide new insights into disease progression, treatment effectiveness, and patient outcomes. These insights can, in turn, lead to the development of new treatments and improvements in healthcare delivery.

EHRs also enable the ability to track and monitor population health, which is essential for managing chronic conditions, detecting and responding to public health concerns, and improving health outcomes on a broad scale. They provide access to public health data, enabling healthcare providers to survey the population for potential health improvements and act as a safety net for potential health threats. EHRs facilitate the efficient collection of data in a form that can be shared across multiple healthcare organizations, enhancing collaboration among healthcare professionals and leading to more coordinated and effective care.

The data collected in EHRs can be leveraged for quality improvement and prevention activities. By analyzing this data, healthcare providers can identify trends, measure the effectiveness of interventions, and develop strategies for improving patient outcomes. Furthermore, EHRs enhance reporting capabilities by making it easier to collect standardized, systematic data. With more and better data available, public health organizations can better monitor, prevent, and manage disease.

EHRs significantly enhance patient engagement and satisfaction in healthcare. They incorporate patient portals and secure online platforms that provide patients with 24-hour access to their health information. These portals allow patients to view their medical history, treatment plans, and test results. This transparency helps patients better understand their health status and care plans, leading to increased engagement.

EHRs also improve communication between patients and healthcare providers. Patients can directly communicate with their healthcare providers to ask questions, request prescription refills, or schedule appointments through secure messaging features. This direct line of communication encourages patients to participate more in their care, improving satisfaction.[10] EHRs also improve workflow by sharing information, reducing paperwork, ensuring accurate information, and providing better patient service.

EHRs play a pivotal role in supporting clinical decision-making. EHRs have the capability to generate reminders, alerts, and notifications, which play a crucial role in preventive care and chronic disease management. These features ensure that patients receive the necessary care at the right time. For example, EHRs can remind healthcare providers when patients are due for preventive screenings or vaccinations. They can also alert healthcare providers when a patient's lab results indicate a potential health risk, enabling timely intervention and management.

EHRs are a significant asset in healthcare, particularly in their capacity to support evidence-based clinical decision-making. They come equipped with evidence-based guidelines and treatment protocols based on the latest clinical research and best practices. These guidelines provide healthcare providers with a reliable basis for making informed decisions about patient care. Using these evidence-based guidelines and protocols can significantly improve the quality of care provided. They ensure that patients receive the most effective treatments based on current medical knowledge.

Furthermore, EHRs ensure that the latest clinical research is readily available to healthcare providers. As new research emerges and guidelines are updated, healthcare providers can stay abreast of the latest developments and incorporate them into their practice.

Integrating these guidelines into EHRs ensures that the latest clinical research is readily available to healthcare providers, promoting the delivery of the most effective and current treatments. This not only improves patient outcomes but also contributes to the overall efficiency and effectiveness of the healthcare system. EHRs are crucial in promoting evidence-based, effective, and efficient healthcare. In essence, EHRs serve as a valuable tool in healthcare, enhancing patient care through improved clinical decision-making, timely interventions, and the provision of evidence-based care.

EHRs provide numerous benefits in healthcare, such as enhancing patient safety, increasing efficiency and productivity, reducing healthcare costs, and supporting clinical decision-making. As healthcare organizations adopt and optimize EHRs, they will become vital in advancing patient outcomes and transforming healthcare delivery (Table 2.1).[10]

Challenges of Using EHRs

Despite their benefits, adopting EHRs in healthcare is challenging. Interoperability means that different systems can share and use data coordinated across different organizations, regions, and countries to provide timely and seamless information portability and improve the health of individuals and populations worldwide.[11] One major challenge is the lack of interoperability between different EHR systems, making it difficult to share patient information between different healthcare providers. This lack of interoperability can lead to errors and delays in patient care, as healthcare providers need access to complete and accurate patient information. Interoperability is essential for delivering high-quality patient care and improving patient outcomes. It allows healthcare providers to share patient information seamlessly, reducing the risk of errors and improving the efficiency of care delivery. However, achieving interoperability can be challenging, as different EHR systems may use different data formats and standards.[11]

Table 2.1   Benefits of EHRs

Benefit	Description
Improving the quality and safety of patient care	EHRs allow for better communication and coordination among healthcare providers, resulting in better patient outcomes and reduced medical errors.
Increasing efficiency and productivity of healthcare providers	EHRs provide a centralized location for storing and accessing patient information, reducing the time and effort required for record-keeping and documentation.
Reducing healthcare costs	EHRs reduce the risk of duplicating tests and procedures, which can lead to significant cost savings for patients and healthcare organizations.
Supporting clinical decision-making	EHRs provide a more comprehensive view of a patient's medical history, allowing healthcare providers to make more informed decisions.
Enhancing patient engagement and satisfaction	EHRs incorporate patient portals, secure online platforms that provide patients with 24-hour access to their health information, leading to increased engagement.
Supporting evidence-based clinical decision-making	EHRs come equipped with evidence-based guidelines and treatment protocols, which are based on the latest clinical research and best practices.

Another challenge with the adoption of EHRs is the privacy and security risks that they pose. EHRs contain sensitive patient information, including demographics, medical history, lab results, and medication records, which must be protected from unauthorized access. The risk of data breaches and cyber-attacks on EHRs is a growing concern as cybercriminals become more sophisticated in their attacks.[12] Unauthorized access to this information can lead to identity theft or fraud.

Also, EHRs are often stored digitally, making them susceptible to data loss or theft. This could occur through various means, such as a data breach or a physical theft of storage devices. EHR systems can also be vulnerable to malware attacks, which can compromise the integrity of the data and potentially lead to unauthorized access or data loss. User errors, such as accidentally deleting records, and design flaws in the EHR system can pose security risks. Furthermore, data breaches can occur when unauthorized individuals access the EHR system. This could lead to the exposure of sensitive patient information. These are some of the risks associated with EHRs that must be carefully managed to ensure the privacy and security of patient data.

To mitigate the risks associated with EHRs, healthcare organizations must ensure their systems are secure and interoperable. This includes implementing robust data security protocols, such as access controls and audit trails, to protect patient information from unauthorized access. Healthcare organizations should educate employees to avoid clicking suspicious links to prevent phishing. Data encryption is another crucial step in protecting and securing EHR data while transferring it between on-site users and external cloud applications.[13]

Risk evaluation is also essential, allowing organizations to assess potential threats before an attack occurs. Using a virtual private network (VPN) with multifactor authentication (MFA) adds an extra layer of security, making it more difficult for unauthorized individuals to access the EHR system. Endpoint detection and response (EDR) systems can help identify potential threats while engaging cyber threat hunters can provide additional expertise in identifying and mitigating potential threats. Finally, conducting Red Team/Blue Team exercises can help identify vulnerabilities and improve security measures. These exercises simulate real-world attacks, allowing organizations to test their defenses and improve their response strategies. When implemented effectively, these measures can significantly enhance the security of EHR systems.

Healthcare organizations must also work to promote interoperability by adopting common data standards and sharing patient information across different EHR systems.[14] Interoperability in healthcare is critical in enhancing patient care and outcomes. It refers to the ability of different information systems, devices, and applications to access, exchange, interpret, and cooperatively use data in a coordinated manner within and across organizational boundaries. Limited interoperability poses a significant challenge for EHR data, as data is rarely standardized.[15]

Healthcare organizations can promote interoperability in several ways. By adopting common data standards, they can ensure that data is consistent, easily shared, and understood across different EHR systems. These standards allow for the seamless exchange of information, reducing the risk of errors and improving the efficiency of care. Sharing patient information across different EHR systems allows for a more comprehensive view of a patient's health history. This can lead to better decision-making and improved patient outcomes.

Promoting interoperability programs, such as the Medicare and Medicaid Promoting Interoperability Programs, encourages healthcare providers to adopt, implement, upgrade, and demonstrate meaningful use of EHR technology.[16] These programs focus on improving patient access to health information and prioritizing interoperability.

A patient-centered interoperability approach ensures patients can access and manage their health information across different platforms. This empowers patients to take an active role in their healthcare and improves patient engagement. Incorporating interoperability into daily operations can improve the efficiency and coordination of care. This includes everything from scheduling appointments to managing patient records.

Connectivity through the internet of things (IoT), such as wearable health monitors, can be integrated with EHR systems to provide real-time patient data. This can enhance patient monitoring and enable proactive care. By promoting interoperability, healthcare organizations can ensure that the correct information is available at the right time to the right people, thereby improving the quality of care and patient outcomes.

In addition to the challenges of interoperability, data privacy, and security, the adoption of EHRs also presents potential risks associated with technology errors. For example, EHRs may contain incorrect or incomplete information due to data entry errors or system malfunctions, leading to medical errors and compromised patient safety. To address this challenge, healthcare organizations must implement processes for verifying the accuracy of EHR data, such as regular audits and data validation checks.

Another challenge associated with the adoption of EHRs is the need for healthcare providers to learn and adapt to new technologies. Many healthcare providers may be resistant to change or unfamiliar with EHR systems, which can lead to slower adoption and implementation of EHRs. To address this challenge, healthcare organizations must provide adequate training and support for healthcare providers to ensure they are comfortable and proficient in using EHR systems. EHRs may also have unintended consequences, such as changes to the workflow of healthcare providers and an increased administrative burden. Healthcare providers may need more time entering data into EHRs and less interaction and communication with patients, which can negatively impact the patient–healthcare provider relationship. Data entry burden and poor usability are top contributors to healthcare provider and nurse dissatisfaction, burnout, and turnover.[17] Healthcare organizations must monitor the impact of EHRs on workflow and continually assess and optimize their EHR systems to minimize any negative consequences.

In conclusion, while EHRs have numerous benefits in healthcare, they also present challenges that must be addressed. Healthcare organizations must implement appropriate data security measures, promote interoperability, and ensure the accuracy and efficiency of EHR systems. They must also provide adequate training and support for healthcare providers and monitor the impact of EHRs on workflow and patient–healthcare provider relationships. By addressing these challenges, healthcare organizations can maximize the benefits of EHRs, improve patient outcomes, and deliver high-quality, patient-centered care.

Using EHRs in Nursing Practice

Nurses play a crucial role in integrating and utilizing EHRs within the healthcare landscape. EHRs have brought about a revolutionary shift in healthcare professionals' management of patient information. By implementing EHR systems, healthcare providers, including nurses, gain expedient and secure access to medical records and other pertinent data, enhancing patient care. Nurses spend more time with patients than other healthcare personnel, so their involvement in EHR adoption and utilization is of utmost importance.

Nurses rely on EHRs to document patient assessments, interventions, and outcomes accurately. These records also facilitate seamless communication with other healthcare providers, promoting efficient collaboration. Nurse utilization of EHRs has proven to significantly reduce medication errors, enhance patient safety, and elevate the quality of care delivered.

One key advantage of EHRs is the provision of timely access to patient information, enabling nurses to make informed decisions regarding patient care. Through EHRs, nurses can readily review a patient's medical history, allergies, and medication list, empowering them to make well-informed choices regarding treatment and care plans. Moreover, the implementation of EHRs fosters collaboration and communication among healthcare providers, a vital component for delivering high-quality care.

To leverage the full potential of EHRs, nurses must receive comprehensive training on their practical use. The first step in effectively using EHRs is learning to access and navigate the system. This involves understanding the system's user interface, knowing where different types of information are stored, and learning how to move between different record sections. Nurses should be able to quickly and efficiently locate patient records, lab results, medication lists, and other relevant information.

Once nurses can navigate the EHR system, they must learn to enter and retrieve data proficiently. This includes entering patient information, updating medical histories, inputting treatment plans, and documenting patient interactions. Additionally, nurses should be able to retrieve data effectively, such as pulling up a patient's medical history or finding lab results. The ability to enter and retrieve data accurately and efficiently is crucial for maintaining up-to-date and comprehensive patient records.

Beyond entering and retrieving data, nurses must also manage electronic documentation proficiently. This involves organizing and maintaining digital files, ensuring that documentation is complete and accurate, and updating records as necessary. Proper electronic documentation management helps ensure that patient records are always up to date, which can improve patient care and increase efficiency. Equipping nurses with these skills ensures they can utilize EHRs optimally, thereby maximizing the associated benefits. EHRs can improve communication between healthcare providers, reduce medical errors, improve patient outcomes, and increase efficiency when used effectively.

Furthermore, they can free up nurses' time for direct patient care by reducing paperwork. Comprehensive training programs are essential for nurses to use EHRs effectively. These programs should encompass various aspects, including accessing and navigating EHR systems, proficiently entering and retrieving data, and managing electronic documentation. With these skills, nurses can fully leverage the potential of EHRs, leading to improved patient care and increased efficiency in healthcare settings.

The ethical and legal considerations surrounding the EHRs are as crucial as the technical aspects. As primary caregivers and frequent users of EHRs, nurses must be aware of these considerations. Patient confidentiality, a fundamental principle in healthcare, must be safeguarded at all times. Nurses must ensure that they only access patient information when necessary for care and do not disclose it without the patient's consent. This includes verbal disclosures and ensuring that EHRs are not left open where others may see them.

In addition to ethical obligations, there are legal requirements for protecting patient information. Laws such as the Health Insurance Portability and Accountability Act (HIPAA) sets strict standards for the security of electronic health information.[1] Nurses must be aware of these laws and ensure that they follow all relevant regulations in their use of EHRs.

Handling sensitive patient information comes with inherent ethical obligations. Nurses must respect patients' privacy rights and protect their information. This includes protecting the information from unauthorized access and ensuring that it is accurate and up to date. Mistakes or omissions in EHRs can lead to severe consequences for patient care.

Nurses play a critical role in the adoption and utilization of EHRs in healthcare. Their role goes beyond simply using the technology; they must also navigate the complex ethical and legal landscape surrounding EHR usage. By doing so, they can help ensure that EHRs are used in a way that benefits patients while also respecting their rights and privacy.

EHR systems have transformed patient data management, providing healthcare professionals with swift and secure access to crucial information. Nurses' involvement in EHR integration enables accurate documentation, effective communication, and improved patient care outcomes. To fully harness the potential benefits of EHRs, nurses should receive comprehensive training on their usage while understanding the ethical and legal implications of their implementation. By embracing EHRs and supporting nurses in their effective utilization, healthcare organizations can cultivate a culture of excellence, benefiting patients and healthcare providers.

Conclusion

EHRs have indeed become a vital component of healthcare delivery. Their adoption has revolutionized how healthcare providers manage patient care, making it more efficient and coordinated. EHRs provide a comprehensive view of a patient's medical history, enabling healthcare providers to make informed decisions about their care.

Despite some challenges, such as initial implementation costs, training, and data security concerns, the benefits of EHRs significantly outweigh these issues. EHRs can improve the quality of care by reducing medical errors, enhancing patient safety, and facilitating care coordination among different healthcare providers. They also increase efficiency by reducing paperwork, making health information readily accessible, and streamlining administrative tasks.

However, to fully realize these benefits, nurses at the forefront of patient care must be well-informed about EHRs and proficient in their use. This includes understanding how to navigate the system, enter and retrieve data accurately, and manage electronic documentation effectively. As the healthcare environment continues to evolve rapidly, with increasing reliance on technology, the role of nurses in managing EHRs becomes even more critical.

In addition to training, ongoing support is essential to help nurses overcome any challenges they may encounter while using EHRs. This could include technical support to resolve system issues, educational resources to keep up with updates or changes to the system, and a feedback mechanism to improve the system based on user experience continually.

In conclusion, while EHRs present some challenges, their benefits to patient care and healthcare delivery are immense. With proper training and support, nurses can effectively use EHRs to deliver high-quality patient care in the rapidly evolving healthcare environment. The future of healthcare is digital, and EHRs are leading the way.

References

1. Amatayakul M. *Electronic Health Records: A Practical Guide for Professionals and Organizations*. Chicago, IL: American Health Information Management, 2007.

2. Detmer DE, Steen EB, Dick RS. (Eds.). *The computer-based patient record: An Essential Technology for Health Care.* Washington, DC: National Academies Press, 1997.
3. Atherton J. Development of the electronic health record. Virt Men. 2011;13(3):186–189. https://doi.org/10.1001/virtualmen tor.2011.13.3.mhst1-1103.
4. Menachemi N, Collum TH. Benefits and drawbacks of electronic health record systems. Risk Manage Healthcare Policy. 2011;4:47–55. doi: 10.2147/RMHP.S12985.
5. Itchhaporia D. The evolution of the quintuple aim: health equity, health outcomes, and the economy. J Am Coll Cardiol. 2021;78(22):2262–2264. doi: 10.1016/j.jacc.2021.10.018. PMID: 34823665; PMCID: PMC8608191.
6. Bodenheimer T, Sinsky C. From triple to Quadruple Aim: care of the patient requires care of the provider. Ann Family Med. 2014;12(6):573–576. https://doi.org/10.1370/afm.1713.
7. Nundy S, Cooper LA, Mate KS. The quintuple aim for health care improvement: a new imperative to advance health equity. JAMA. 2022;327(6):521–522. https://doi.org/10.1001/jama.2021.25181.
8. Scott J. *Become an Insider | Sign up Today to Receive Premium Content! Latest Articles Quintuple Aim: What Is It, and How Can Technology Help Achieve It?,* 2023.
9. Farrell TW, Greer AG, Bennie S, Hageman H, Pfeifle A. Academic health centers and the Quintuple Aim of health care. Acad Med. 2023;98(5):563–568. https://doi.org/10.1097/ACM.0000000000005031
10. Brands MR, Gouw SC, Beestrum M, Cronin RM, Fijnvandraat K, Badawy SM. Patient-centered digital health records and their effects on health outcomes: systematic review. J Med Internet Res. 2022;24(12):e43086. https://doi.org/10.2196/43086
11. Interoperability in Healthcare, n.d. HIMSS. Retrieved November 23, 2023, from www.himss.org/resources/interoperability-hea lthcare
12. Cybersecurity in Healthcare, n.d. HIMSS. Retrieved November 23, 2023, from Cybersecurity in Healthcare. Cybersecurity in Healthcare | HIMSS.
13. del Prado R. *Understanding EHR privacy and security,* 2023. Retrieved from www.healthcareinformation.management/ele ctronic-health-records-ehr-systems-ehr-privacy-and-security.

14. Snell E. *Data security considerations in healthcare interoperability*, 2017. Retrieved from Mitigating Barriers to Interoperability in Health Care | HIMSS.

15. Kruse CS, Goswamy R, Raval Y, Marawi S. Challenges and opportunities of big data in health care: a systematic review. JMIR Medical Informatics. 2016;4(4):1–11. https://doi.org/10.2196/medinform.5359

16. Promoting Interoperability Programs, 2022. Retrieved from www.federalregister.gov/documents/2022/08/10/2022-16472/medicare-program-hospital-inpatient-prospective-payment-systems-for-acute-care-hospitals-and-the.

17. Henry TA. *7 EHR usability, safety challenges—and how to overcome them*, 2018. Retrieved from www.ama-assn.org/practice-management/digital/7-ehr-usability-safety-challenges-and-how-overcome-them.

Chapter 3

Health Information Exchange (HIE)

Importance of Health Information Exchange (HIE)

In today's healthcare landscape, patients receive care from a diverse range of healthcare providers in various settings, such as hospitals, clinics, and long-term care facilities. As a result, there is an increasing need for effective communication and collaboration among healthcare providers to ensure that patients receive quality care that is continuous and comprehensive. In addition, it is crucial to have a reliable and secure method for sharing patient information among healthcare providers to ensure there is continuity of care.

HIE is a process that allows for the secure and seamless exchange of patient health information between healthcare

DOI: 10.4324/9781003439721-3

providers, regardless of the location or setting of care.[1] HIE enables healthcare providers to access patient information such as medical history, medication lists, lab results, and other essential health data, regardless of the location or setting of care. By leveraging HIE, healthcare providers can quickly and easily share patient information, reducing the risk of medical errors and improving patient outcomes. HIE also helps to eliminate duplication of tests and procedures, which can be time-consuming and costly. Avoiding unnecessary tests and procedures can save time and money.

One significant advantage of HIE is its ability to facilitate the coordination of care among healthcare providers. For example, a primary care physician can share a patient's medical records with a specialist to ensure that the specialist has all the necessary information to provide appropriate treatment. HIE can also help healthcare providers identify potential medication interactions, allergies, and other health-related issues that may affect patient care.

Moreover, HIE can play a crucial role in emergency situations. In emergencies, healthcare providers need quick access to vital patient information to make informed decisions about treatment. HIE can help healthcare providers quickly access vital information, such as allergies, medication lists, and pre-existing medical conditions, which can help them provide the appropriate treatment in a timely manner.

HIE is a valuable tool to ensure continuity of care, improve patient outcomes, and enhance effective communication and collaboration among healthcare providers. With the increasing adoption of electronic health records and the growing demand for integrated and coordinated care, HIE is becoming more critical than ever in today's healthcare landscape.

Benefits of HIE

HIE is a beneficial and impactful technology for both healthcare providers and patients. It enables the secure and efficient exchange of patient health information, leading to better care coordination, fewer medical errors, enhanced patient safety, and more informed clinical decision-making. HIE enables healthcare providers to access a patient's complete medical history, including test results, medication history, allergies, and other vital information. This information helps healthcare providers to provide timely and appropriate care to patients. Other benefits include fewer procedure duplication, reduced medical imaging, and lower costs.[2]

HIE also facilitates care coordination. In today's complex healthcare system, patients often receive care from multiple healthcare providers and in different settings. With HIE, healthcare providers can communicate and coordinate care more effectively, resulting in a more integrated and seamless healthcare experience for patients. By having access to updated patient information, healthcare providers can avoid care delays and ensure that patients receive the proper care when they need it.

Another benefit of HIE is improved public health surveillance. HIE allows healthcare providers to track and monitor health trends and outbreaks, enabling faster responses and better public health outcomes. Additionally, HIE can lead to cost savings by reducing unnecessary procedures and improving care coordination, leading to fewer hospital readmissions and shorter hospital stays.

In summary, HIE offers significant benefits for both healthcare providers and patients, including improved care coordination, reduced medical errors, enhanced patient safety, and more informed clinical decision-making. As the healthcare industry continues to evolve, HIE will play a crucial role in providing high-quality, patient-centered care (Table 3.1).

Table 3.1   Benefits of HIE

Benefit of HIE	Benefit Explained
Improved patient care coordination	HIE enables healthcare providers to exchange and coordinate care information more effectively, resulting in an efficient and connected healthcare journey for patients. By having access to current patient information, healthcare providers can prevent care gaps and ensure that patients get the right care at the right time. HIE also facilitates the transfer of care across different locations, such as from hospital to home or from primary care to specialty care.[1]
Reduced medical errors and increased patient safety	HIE helps to reduce medical errors and improve patient safety by providing healthcare providers with access to complete and accurate patient information. By having this information readily available, healthcare providers can avoid duplicating tests and procedures, which can lead to unnecessary costs and risks to patients. Additionally, HIE can help identify potential medication interactions and allergies, reducing the risk of adverse drug events. HIE can also help prevent errors in patient identification, such as mixing up patient records or assigning the wrong treatment.[2]
More informed clinical decision-making	HIE allows healthcare providers to make more informed clinical decisions and offer more customized care. By accessing a patient's full medical history, healthcare providers can have a better grasp of the patient's situation, desires, and requirements. HIE can also help healthcare providers obtain evidence-based recommendations and best practices, which can help them deliver the most suitable and effective treatment. HIE can also enable collaborative decision-making between healthcare providers and patients, which can enhance patient satisfaction and involvement.[3]

(continued)

Table 3.1   (Continued)

Benefit of HIE	Benefit Explained
Improved public health surveillance and outcomes	HIE enables healthcare providers to track and monitor health trends and outbreaks, allowing for faster responses and better public health outcomes. With HIE, healthcare providers can monitor and report on infectious diseases, chronic conditions, immunizations, and other public health issues. HIE can also help healthcare providers access population health data and analytics, which can help them identify health disparities and gaps in care, and design interventions to improve health equity and quality.[1]
Cost savings and efficiency	HIE can lead to cost savings and efficiency by reducing unnecessary procedures and improving care coordination, leading to fewer hospital readmissions and shorter hospital stays. HIE can also help healthcare providers optimize the use of resources, such as staff, equipment, and supplies, by improving workflow and reducing administrative burden. HIE can also help reduce healthcare fraud and abuse, by providing a more transparent and accountable system for billing and reimbursement.[1]

[1] HIE Benefits, n.d. HealhtIT.Gov. Retrieved November 24, 2023, from www.healthit.gov/topic/health-it-and-health-information-exchange-basics/hie-benefits.

[2] AHIMA. HIE management and operational considerations. J AHIMA. 2011;82(5): 56–61.

[3] Health Data Management Data Exchange HIE HSSC Interoperability Investment Returns on Population Health Quality of Care, n.d. Retrieved November 24, 2023, from www.healthdatamanagement.com/articles/how-health-info-exchanges-and-data-utilities-are-returning-demonstrable-benefits.

Challenges of HIE

While HIE offers numerous benefits, it is not without its challenges. One of the most significant challenges is the need for more standardization and consistency of healthcare data across different healthcare settings and systems.[3] Healthcare data is often stored in different formats, making it difficult to store, share, and integrate patient information. This can result in incomplete or inaccurate patient data, leading to medical errors and suboptimal patient care.

Another challenge of HIE is ensuring the privacy and security of patient information during its exchange. There is a significant risk of unauthorized access to sensitive patient information during transmission, which can result in identity theft or other privacy breaches. Healthcare providers must comply with strict regulations and rigorous rules such as the Health Insurance Portability and Accountability Act (HIPAA)[4,5] to ensure the confidentiality and integrity of patient data.

Additionally, there may be resistance to the adoption of HIE among healthcare providers due to concerns about workflow disruption and increased administrative burden. The implementation of HIE requires significant investment in time, resources, and infrastructure. Healthcare providers must learn new technologies and processes to incorporate HIE into their workflow, which can be challenging and time-consuming.

Another difficulty of HIE is the possible incompatibility between different healthcare information systems, which can affect the effective sharing of patient information. This can be particularly troublesome in areas where patients receive care from multiple healthcare providers or healthcare systems. Another challenge of HIE is the need for more patient engagement in the process. Patients may need to be made aware of HIE and its advantages, or they may be concerned about the privacy and security of their health information. Building patient trust and understanding of the process is essential for the success of HIE (Table 3.2).

To sum up, HIE has many advantages for healthcare providers and patients, but it also has some difficulties. These difficulties, such as the standardization of healthcare data,

Table 3.2   Themes Associated with Challenges for Big Data in Healthcare

Themes	Examples
Data structure	This theme encompasses issues related to the fragmented nature of healthcare data, incompatible data formats, heterogeneous data sources, raw and unstructured datasets, large volumes of data, high variety and velocity of data, lack of transparency, and security concerns
Security	Includes sub-themes such as privacy, confidentiality, data duplication, integrity, and the need for data standardization
Data standardization	Challenges related to data acquisition and cleansing, global sharing of data, terminology standardization, and language barriers
Storage and transfers	Focuses on the expensive nature of storing healthcare data, transferring data from one place to another, securely storing electronic data, and extracting, transmitting, and processing data securely
Managerial issues	Includes governance issues, ownership concerns, and the lack of skilled personnel to handle big data in healthcare
Lack of skill	Highlights the challenges associated with having personnel who are not adequately trained to work with big data in healthcare
Inaccuracies	Inconsistences, lack of precision and data timeliness
Regulatory compliance	Legal concerns
Real-time analytics	Need for real-time analysis in healthcare

Source: Kruse CS, Goswamy R, Raval Y, Marawi S. Challenges and opportunities of big data in health care: a systematic review. JMIR Med Inform. 2016;4(4):e38. doi: 10.2196/medinform.5359. PMID: 27872036; PMCID: PMC5138448.

Note: The table provides a comprehensive overview of the various challenges and themes associated with big data in healthcare, highlighting the complexity and multifaceted nature of working with large datasets in this field.

privacy and security issues, and interoperability problems, must be resolved to achieve effective implementation and adoption of HIE. Healthcare providers must also address concerns around workflow disruption and involve patients to ensure their awareness and confidence in the process. With adequate planning and execution, HIE can lead to improved patient care and better health outcomes.

Using HIE in Nursing Practice

In today's complex healthcare landscape, patients may receive care from multiple healthcare providers in different healthcare settings. As a result, there is a critical need for healthcare providers to have access to a patient's complete medical history to ensure continuity of care. This is where HIE plays a vital role in healthcare delivery, as it facilitates the seamless exchange of patient information between healthcare providers, regardless of the location or setting of care.

HIE is a transformative tool in modern healthcare, particularly in nursing practice. By ensuring all healthcare providers involved in a patient's care have access to the same information, HIE significantly improves the coordination of patient care. This leads to more consistent and efficient care as healthcare providers can seamlessly share and update patient information, reducing the risk of miscommunication or information gaps that could impact patient care.

Providing healthcare providers with complete and accurate patient information is a key advantage of HIE. This can significantly reduce medical errors, a critical aspect of patient safety. For instance, HIE can prevent medication errors by alerting healthcare providers to potential drug interactions or allergies. This real-time alert system can help nurses avoid adverse drug events, enhancing patient safety.

Furthermore, HIE enhances patient safety by providing real-time access to patient information. It enables nurses and other healthcare providers to make immediate and informed decisions, reducing the risk of treatment delays or errors.

Having access to a patient's complete medical history allows healthcare providers to make better-informed decisions about treatment plans. For nurses, this means being able to provide personalized care based on a comprehensive understanding of the patient's health status. It also supports evidence-based nursing practice, as nurses can use the wealth of data available through HIE to inform their care strategies and interventions.

The impact of HIE on nurses is profound, as it directly influences their daily responsibilities and interactions with patients. With HIE, nurses can access a patient's complete medical history, including previous diagnoses, treatments, and medications. This comprehensive view allows nurses to coordinate care more effectively, ensuring that all healthcare providers involved in a patient's care are on the same page.

By providing accurate and up-to-date patient information, HIE reduces the likelihood of medical errors. For instance, nurses can check a patient's medication history to avoid harmful drug interactions or allergies, thereby enhancing patient safety. By having immediate access to a patient's health records, nurses can make informed decisions about patient care. This can prevent unnecessary procedures or tests, reducing the risk of complications and improving patient safety.

HIE provides nurses with a wealth of information that can inform their clinical decision-making. For example, a nurse can review a patient's past responses to treatments when planning future care. This leads to more personalized and effective care. With HIE, nurses spend less time tracking down patient information and more time providing direct patient care. This not only improves efficiency but also allows nurses to focus on their primary responsibility of caring for patients.

HIE can also facilitate patient engagement. Nurses can use the information from HIE to educate patients about their health conditions and treatment plans, promoting patient involvement in their own care. In summary, HIE significantly impacts nursing by enhancing patient care coordination, reducing medical errors, improving patient safety, informing clinical decision-making, increasing efficiency, and promoting patient engagement. It equips nurses with the tools and information they need to provide the best possible care to their patients.

While HIE has the potential to revolutionize healthcare delivery, its adoption is not without challenges. One of the major challenges is the lack of standardization of healthcare data across different healthcare settings and systems. Healthcare data can be incredibly diverse, ranging from clinical notes and laboratory results to imaging studies and patient-reported outcomes. Each healthcare provider or institution may use different systems, formats, or terminologies to record and store this data. This lack of standardization can make it difficult to exchange and integrate data seamlessly through HIE. It can lead to inconsistencies, misinterpretations, and errors, which can ultimately impact patient care. Efforts are needed to develop and adopt standardized data formats, terminologies, and protocols to facilitate effective data exchange.

Protecting the privacy and security of patient information during its exchange is another critical challenge. The exchange of health information across different healthcare settings increases the risk of data breaches and unauthorized access to sensitive patient information. This can potentially lead to violations of patient privacy and loss of trust in the healthcare system. Therefore, robust security measures, including data encryption, secure user authentication, and strict access controls, need to be in place to protect patient data during its exchange. Additionally, policies and procedures need to be developed to ensure compliance with data privacy laws and regulations, such as the HIPAA in the United States.

Addressing these challenges is crucial for the successful implementation and adoption of HIE. It requires collaborative efforts from healthcare providers, IT professionals, policymakers, and other stakeholders in the healthcare industry. Despite these challenges, the benefits of HIE in improving patient care coordination, reducing medical errors, and enhancing patient safety make it a worthwhile endeavor.

The adoption of HIE can lead to concerns about workflow disruption and an increased administrative burden, particularly for nurses who are often at the forefront of patient care.

The integration of HIE into existing workflows can necessitate changes in work processes and routines. For instance, instead of relying on paper-based records or disparate electronic systems, healthcare providers would need to use the HIE system to access and share patient information. This shift can disrupt established workflows, at least initially, until healthcare providers become accustomed to the new system. Some healthcare providers may resist this change, particularly if they perceive the new system as more complex or time-consuming than their current practices.

The effective use of HIE may also require additional tasks, which can increase the administrative burden on nurses. These tasks can include data entry, as patient information must be accurately entered into the system. Verification tasks are also necessary to ensure the accuracy and completeness of the data. Furthermore, the management of the HIE system, such as maintaining patient consent forms for data sharing and ensuring the system is used appropriately, can also fall to nurses. These additional tasks can increase the workload of nurses, competing with direct patient care tasks.

However, it is important to note that while the adoption of HIE can present challenges, many of these can be mitigated with appropriate strategies. For instance, providing comprehensive training can ease the transition to new workflows, helping healthcare providers become comfortable with the HIE system. Similarly, the administrative burden can be reduced by implementing efficient data entry and management processes and by leveraging features of the HIE system that are designed to streamline tasks. Despite the challenges, the benefits of HIE, including improved patient care coordination, reduced medical errors, and enhanced patient safety, make it a valuable tool in modern healthcare.

Nurses play a crucial role in the implementation and use of HIE in healthcare. HIE can enhance nursing practice by providing timely and accurate patient information, enabling nurses to make better-informed clinical decisions and improve patient outcomes. Nurses can use HIE to obtain important patient information such as medication lists, allergies, and medical histories, which can be vital in providing safe and effective care. HIE can also assist nurses in identifying gaps in patient care and fostering communication and collaboration among different healthcare providers involved in a patient's care. By using HIE, nurses can enhance the quality and continuity of care for their patients.

However, nurses must also ensure the security and privacy of patient information during its exchange. This involves adhering to rigorous protocols and procedures to ensure that patient data is accessed only by authorized personnel and that patient confidentiality is maintained. Nurses must also understand the ethical and legal implications associated with using HIE, such as informed consent, confidentiality, and patient autonomy.

Furthermore, nurses must be familiar with the technology that enables HIE, including how to navigate electronic health records and interpret patient data. Nurses should receive adequate training on the use of HIE systems to ensure they can use them effectively and efficiently. Nurses can also play a vital role in educating patients about HIE, explaining the benefits and potential challenges, and ensuring that patients understand their rights related to their health information.

HIE is a powerful tool that can enhance nursing practice in numerous ways. From improving care coordination and reducing medical errors to enhancing patient safety and supporting informed clinical decision-making, HIE plays a pivotal role in delivering high-quality, patient-centered care. As healthcare continues to evolve, the use of tools like HIE in nursing practice will continue to grow in importance.

Conclusion

In conclusion, HIE is an essential component of healthcare delivery, enabling the exchange of patient information between healthcare providers and improving patient care coordination. Despite the challenges associated with its use, the benefits of HIE are substantial, and its adoption is necessary to provide high-quality patient care. Nurses play a crucial role in the successful implementation and adoption of HIE. They are often the primary users of patient information, and their understanding and effective use of HIE are critical to its success. Therefore, it is essential that nurses receive adequate training on the use of HIE. This includes understanding how to access and interpret information from the HIE, as well as how to input patient data and information accurately and efficiently.

By addressing the challenges associated with HIE adoption, healthcare providers can ensure that patients receive the best possible care and achieve better health outcomes. Despite the challenges associated with its use, the adoption of HIE is a necessary step towards improving healthcare delivery. By understanding the relevance of HIE and effectively using it in their practice, nurses can contribute significantly to this undertaking. Addressing the challenges associated with HIE adoption will ensure that patients receive the best possible care, leading to improved health outcomes. The journey may be challenging, but the destination is undoubtedly worthwhile.

References

1. Williams C, Mostashari F, Mertz K, Hogin E, Atwal P. From the Office of the National Coordinator: the strategy for advancing the exchange of health information. Health Aff (Millwood). 2012;31(3):527–536. doi: 10.1377/hlthaff.2011.1314. Erratum in: Health Aff (Millwood). 2012;31(3):886. PMID: 22392663.
2. Menachemi N, Rahurkar S, Harle CA, Vest JR. The benefits of health information exchange: an updated systematic review. J Am Med Inform Assoc. 2018;25(9):1259–1265. doi: 10.1093/jamia/ocy035. PMID: 29718258; PMCID: PMC7646861.
3. Kruse CS, Goswamy R, Raval Y, Marawi S. Challenges and opportunities of big data in health care: A systematic review. JMIR Medical Informatics. 2016;4(4): 1–11. https://doi.org/10.2196/medinform.5359.
4. Summary of the HIPAA Privacy Rule, n.d. Retrieved November 24, 2023, from www.hhs.gov/hipaa/for-professionals/privacy/laws-regulations/index.html.
5. Health Insurance Portability and Accountability Act of 1996 (HIPAA), June 27, 2022. Retrieved from Health Insurance Portability and Accountability Act of 1996 (HIPAA) | Public Health Law | CDC.

Chapter 4

Clinical Decision Support Systems (CDSSs)

History and Evolution of Clinical Decision Support Systems

Clinical decision support systems (CDSSs) have a rich history that dates to the 1980s. At the time, the primary focus was developing simple rule-based decision-making systems. These early systems relied on predefined rules to provide recommendations to healthcare providers. However, they were limited in handling complex data and required manual updating to keep pace with the rapidly evolving medical knowledgebase.[1]

Over time, CDSSs evolved into more sophisticated systems integrating advanced computing techniques such as machine

DOI: 10.4324/9781003439721-4

learning and natural language processing. These techniques allowed CDSSs to handle complex data sets, learn from patient data over time, and provide more personalized recommendations to healthcare providers. CDSSs that use natural language processing (NLP) can extract vital information from patient electronic health records (EHRs) to help with critical decision-support tasks.[2] NLP is a technique that enables computers to understand and process human language, such as text and speech. Using NLP, CDSSs can analyze patient EHRs containing rich and diverse information about the patient's health history, condition, treatment, and outcomes.[2] CDSS can use this information to provide valuable recommendations to healthcare providers, such as diagnosis, treatment, prevention, and monitoring (Figure 4.1).

Today, CDSS has become a crucial component of clinical decision-making, providing healthcare providers with real-time information to guide their decisions. CDSSs can help

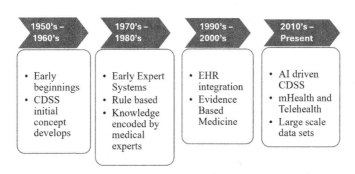

Figure 4.1 The history of CDSS. (Modified from Chen, Z, Liang N, Zhang H, Li H, Yang Y, Zong X, Chen Y, Wang Y, Shi N. Harnessing the power of clinical decision support systems: challenges and opportunities. Open Heart. 2023;10(2)):1–11. https://doi.org/10.1136/openhrt-2023-002432.)

clinicians with various tasks such as diagnosis, treatment planning, medication management, and monitoring of patient outcomes. It can alert clinicians to potential drug interactions, suggest appropriate diagnostic tests, and recommend evidence-based treatments. CDSS has been shown to improve patient outcomes by reducing medical errors, improving diagnostic accuracy, and optimizing treatment plans.[3] These systems have also been shown to reduce healthcare costs by minimizing unnecessary tests, procedures, and hospitalizations (Figure 4.2).

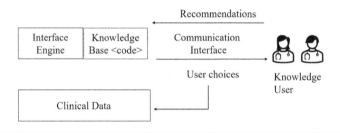

Figure 4.2   Diagram of knowledge-based single system CDSS. (Modified from Sutton RT, Pincock D, Baumgart DC, Sadowski, DC, Fedorak RN, Kroeker, KI An overview of clinical decision support systems: benefits, risks, and strategies for success. NPJ Digit Med. 2020;3:17. https://doi. org/10.1038/s41746-020-0221-y.)

Knowledge-based clinical decision support systems (CDSS) are developed using a knowledgebase that comprises a collection of data organized in the form of if–then rules. These rules, also known as if–then statements, are designed to assess the data and generate a specific action or outcome. The creation of these rules relies on various sources of knowledge, including practice-based evidence, literature-based evidence, and patient-directed evidence. This approach enables the CDSS to leverage a comprehensive knowledgebase to assist healthcare professionals in making informed decisions and providing optimal care to patients

Benefits of CDSS

CDSS offers many advantages that can enhance the quality of care and increase the efficiency of healthcare delivery. One of the most significant benefits is improved patient outcomes. CDSS can improve communication and collaboration among healthcare providers and reduce variability in clinical decision-making. CDSS provides healthcare providers with timely information and evidence-based recommendations that can result in more accurate diagnoses, appropriate treatments, and better patient outcomes.[4] CDSS can also help healthcare providers stay updated with the latest evidence-based practices and clinical guidelines, leading to more informed clinical decision-making.

CDSS offers many benefits, one of the most significant being the reduction of medical errors.[5] CDSS minimizes the chances of oversight or misdiagnosis by providing data-driven insights, enhancing healthcare services' quality.[5] CDSS can detect potential adverse drug reactions, crucial in preventing medication errors. It does this by cross-referencing patient data with a vast drug interactions and contraindications database.[1] The system can identify potential interactions by analyzing a patient's medication regimen in real time. If a potential issue is detected, the system can alert clinicians, who can decide whether further testing is needed or if a referral to a specialist is appropriate.

Errors in diagnosis, treatment, and medication management can lead to serious adverse events, including hospitalization and even death. CDSS helps minimize these errors by providing healthcare providers timely alerts and reminders. This feature is particularly useful in busy clinical settings with high oversight risk.

CDSS also plays a crucial role in improving compliance with clinical guidelines. Integrating these guidelines into the system, CDSS ensures that healthcare providers are continually updated with the latest best practices. This improves the quality of care and enhances patient safety. CDSS is a powerful tool that can significantly improve patient care by reducing medical errors, detecting adverse drug reactions, improving compliance with clinical guidelines, and reducing the risk of adverse drug interactions.

CDSSs not only improve patient outcomes and reduce medical errors but they also enhance the efficiency of healthcare delivery. By simplifying or automating routine tasks and providing healthcare providers with relevant information at the point of care, CDSSs can reduce the time spent on administrative tasks and optimize workflow.[4] Improved workflows lead to better utilization of resources, increased patient throughput, and, ultimately, improved patient satisfaction. CDSS provides healthcare providers with relevant, real-time information at the point of care. This immediate access to information helps healthcare providers make informed decisions quickly, further enhancing the efficiency of healthcare delivery. CDSS is crucial in keeping healthcare providers updated with the latest evidence-based practices and clinical guidelines. CDSS can be designed to provide alerts and reminders based on current clinical guidelines, ensuring that healthcare providers are using the most appropriate and effective treatments.[6]

Clinical decision-making is improved, and variability in clinical practice is reduced, leading to improved quality of care. CDSS is a powerful tool that can help clinical decision-making, reduce practice variability, and improve care quality.

CDSS plays a significant role in enhancing communication and collaboration among healthcare providers. CDSS enables seamless communication between healthcare providers across different settings and specialties by providing a platform for sharing patient information and clinical decision-making.

This enhanced communication is crucial in improving the continuity of care. When healthcare providers share comprehensive patient information, they can deliver more consistent and coordinated care.[7] This is particularly important for patients with complex conditions who may see multiple specialists.

CDSS can help reduce the duplication of services. When all healthcare providers involved in a patient's care have access to the same information, they can avoid repeating tests or procedures that have already been done. This not only saves resources but also spares patients from unnecessary procedures.[7]

Finally, by enhancing communication and collaboration, CDSS can improve patients' overall quality of care. With more accurate and comprehensive information, healthcare providers can make better-informed decisions, leading to more effective treatments and improved patient outcomes. CDSS is a powerful tool for enhancing communication and collaboration among healthcare providers, leading to improved continuity of care, reduced duplication of services, and improved quality of care.

In summary, CDSS has numerous benefits that can improve care quality and enhance healthcare delivery efficiency. CDSS can improve patient outcomes, reduce medical errors, increase efficiency, improve communication and collaboration, and help healthcare providers stay updated with the latest evidence-based practices and clinical guidelines.

Challenges of CDSS

The integration of CDSS into clinical workflows is challenging. One significant challenge is workflow misalignment. This refers to the difficulties that arise when the CDSS does not align well with the existing clinical workflows. If the CDSSs, especially those empowered by artificial intelligence (AI), are not integrated seamlessly into existing workflows, it can disrupt established processes and lead to inefficiencies. These systems are designed to provide patient-specific recommendations to improve clinical work. However, disruptions and inefficiencies can occur if they do not align with the existing clinical processes.[8]

Another challenge is user acceptance. The success of CDSS interventions largely depends on clinicians' acceptance of them. If the system does not fit into their established workflow or requires significant changes to their routine, it may face resistance. Technical limitations of CDSS, such as poor system integration or time-intensive operations, can also lead to workflow misalignment.[8] Additionally, environmental factors, such as the physical layout of the clinical setting or the availability of necessary hardware and software, can impact the alignment of CDSS with clinical workflows.

Addressing these issues requires a deep understanding of the clinical workflow at multiple levels, emergent processes, and contextual factors. This understanding can help design CDSSs that are better aligned with the workflow, improving their effectiveness and acceptance.

Successful implementation and utilization of CDSS in healthcare are complex and challenging. One key challenge is interpreting and acting on the recommendations provided by the CDSS. This could be due to various reasons, such as poor uptake, inappropriate use, unintended consequences, and technology abandonment over time. The complexity of converting clinical logic into computer-executable algorithms, which requires skills in medicine and informatics, can also pose a challenge.

The quality and accuracy of the data used by CDSS are crucial for its effectiveness. Challenges related to data quality and accuracy can arise from various sources. For instance, non-knowledge-based CDSS, which leverage AI, machine learning (ML), or statistical pattern recognition, often need help understanding the logic that AI uses to produce recommendations and problems with data availability. Furthermore, there may be challenges in interpreting and acting on CDSS recommendations related to the quality and accuracy of the data used by CDSS.[9]

Alert fatigue describes a situation where healthcare providers, after receiving too many alerts or reminders, begin to override or ignore further alerts without attending to them. This phenomenon occurs because of the sheer number of alerts, compounded by the fact that the vast majority of alerts generated by CDSS are clinically inconsequential.[10] This can lead to potential medical errors and compromise patient safety. The most significant barrier to using CDSSs is an increased workload.[11]

CDSS handles sensitive patient data, which must be protected from unauthorized access or disclosure. This includes individually identifiable health information, which is defined as "information that relates to the past, present, or future physical or mental health or condition of an individual; the provision of health care to an individual; or the past, present, or future payment for the provision of health care to an individual".[12] Any identifying non-health information added to a designated record set also assumes the same privacy protections.[12] Therefore, it is crucial that CDSS have robust privacy measures in place to ensure that patient data is handled appropriately and confidentially.

The security of patient data is another significant concern. CDSS must ensure that patient information is stored and transmitted securely. This can be achieved through various means, such as implementing strict access rights, using advanced cryptography for data encryption during transmission and storage, and ensuring that the systems are designed with security in mind.[13] CDSS offers many benefits but presents data privacy and security challenges. These systems must be designed and implemented with these considerations in mind to protect sensitive patient data and maintain trust in the system. It is essential to note that solutions to these challenges are being actively researched and implemented to maximize the benefits of CDSS in healthcare while minimizing potential risks.

Another challenge is the need for more standardization in CDSS. CDSS may use different algorithms, data sources, and decision-making processes, leading to variability in recommendations and clinical outcomes. This variability can lead to unwarranted variations in care, such as overtreatment and lack of adherence to guidelines, which can harm outcomes.[14] CDSS applications that use evidence-based guidelines and AI are designed to ensure personalized and standardized care, leading to optimal outcomes. Standardization of CDSS can improve consistency and quality of care. By making the basis for decisions explicit, widening available information, and encouraging more consistent decisions, CDSS can reduce unwarranted variation in processes and patient outcomes.[14] This can lead to improved efficiency and quality of patient care, including the safety of medication prescribing, use of preventative care in hospitalized patients, access to accurate medical records, patient–physician communication, and adherence to guideline-based care. Standardization can also reduce variability.[1] Through reducing unwarranted variation, CDSS may reduce the inappropriate use of healthcare resources without compromising patient outcomes. However, the full realization of these downstream consequences has been hampered by mixed reports of CDSS adherence, leading to uncertainty about their impacts on patient and health system outcomes.

Standardization of CDSS can enhance interoperability.[15] Interoperability allows different systems and applications to communicate, enabling healthcare providers to access and integrate information regardless of the system in which the data is stored. Enforcing interoperability standards mitigates one of the critical challenges for CDSS: getting information from different systems. CDSS is only as good as the data or information that goes into the system. While CDSS offers many benefits, it also presents challenges related to the need for more standardization. These systems must be designed and implemented with these considerations in mind to improve consistency and quality of care, reduce variability, and enhance interoperability.

Finally, the cost of implementing and maintaining CDSS can be significant, especially for smaller healthcare organizations.[16] However, it is essential to note that the costs can vary widely depending on the specific CDSS, the healthcare setting, and the scope of the implementation.[17] Smaller healthcare organizations may face particular challenges in implementing CDSS due to limited resources. The high costs associated with acquiring, implementing, and maintaining CDSS can be a significant barrier for these organizations.[18] Also, smaller organizations may need more technical expertise to implement and maintain these systems effectively.

Healthcare providers must also invest in training and education to ensure the effective use of CDSS in clinical decision-making.[18] Healthcare providers need to understand how to use the system effectively, interpret its recommendations, and integrate them into their clinical decision-making process. This requires ongoing training and education, which can add to the overall cost of implementing CDSS.

In conclusion, while CDSS has numerous benefits in improving patient outcomes, reducing medical errors, and increasing efficiency in healthcare delivery, it also faces several challenges, including integration into clinical workflows, ethical concerns, data quality, and security, alert fatigue, lack of standardization, and cost. It is imperative for healthcare providers to meticulously evaluate the pros and cons of CDSS and strive to mitigate these issues to guarantee the secure and efficient application of CDSS in clinical decision-making.

Using CDSS in Nursing Practice

Nurses need to use CDSS in practice to enhance patient care. Nurses and nurse informaticists have a critical role in successfully implementing and effectively using CDSS. CDSS provides valuable tools and resources that can support nurses in making informed decisions and providing high-quality care to their patients. Nurses have a deep understanding of the unique needs and challenges faced by patients in various healthcare settings. By collaborating with nurse informaticists who possess specialized knowledge in healthcare information technology and data management, nurses can actively contribute to developing, customizing, and integrating CDSS into their practice (Table 4.1).

CDSS enables nurses to access real-time patient information, including clinical guidelines and recommendations, assisting them in making informed decisions regarding patient care. However, nurses must also be aware of the limitations of CDSS and know how to interpret and apply the recommendations based on individual

Table 4.1   Recommendations on Successful Implementation of CDSS

Strong leadership and stakeholder engagement	Ensure strong leadership support for the implementation of CDSS, with active involvement from key stakeholders such as healthcare administrators, clinicians, and IT professionals. Establish clear roles and responsibilities for each stakeholder group to foster collaboration and shared accountability.
Needs assessment and system customization	Conduct a thorough needs assessment to identify specific areas where CDSS can have the most impact. Tailor the CDSS to meet the unique requirements and workflows of the healthcare organization, taking into account the preferences and needs of end-users.
User training and support	Provide comprehensive training programs to educate healthcare providers on the functionality and benefits of CDSS. Offer ongoing technical support and assistance to address any issues or concerns that may arise during the implementation and usage of the system.
Seamless integration with existing systems	Ensure seamless integration of CDSS with existing electronic health record (EHR) systems and other clinical applications. Aim for interoperability and data exchange capabilities to enable smooth communication and information sharing between different systems.
Continuous evaluation and improvement	Establish mechanisms for ongoing evaluation of CDSS effectiveness and usability. Solicit feedback from end-users to identify areas for improvement and make necessary adjustments to optimize the system's performance.

(*continued*)

Table 4.1 (Continued)

Privacy and security considerations	Implement robust security measures to protect patient data and ensure compliance with privacy regulations. Maintain strict access controls and encryption protocols to safeguard sensitive information within the CDSS.
Change management and communication	Implement effective change management strategies to manage resistance and facilitate the adoption of CDSS. Communicate the goals, benefits, and progress of the CDSS implementation to all stakeholders, fostering transparency and a shared understanding of the system's value.
Collaboration and knowledge-sharing	Foster collaboration and knowledge-sharing among healthcare professionals and organizations that have successfully implemented CDSS. Promote the exchange of best practices, lessons learned, and success stories to facilitate the widespread adoption of CDSS.

Source: Sutton RT, Pincock D, Baumgart DC, Sadowski DC, Fedorak RN, Kroeker KI. An overview of clinical decision support systems: benefits, risks, and strategies for success. NPJ Digit Med. 2020;3:17. doi: 10.1038/s41746-020-0221-y. PMID: 32047862; PMCID: PMC7005290.

Note: By following these recommendations, healthcare organizations can promote the successful implementation of CDSS, leading to improved clinical decision-making, enhanced patient care, and better health outcomes.

patient needs and preferences. In nursing practice, CDSS offers several benefits. Nurses can use it to monitor patient vital signs and receive alerts and notifications for potential abnormalities, helping prevent adverse events such as sepsis.[16] CDSS also assists in identifying potential medication interactions, dosage errors, or allergies, allowing nurses to adjust medication orders and ensure patient safety. CDSS supports nurses in prioritizing and triaging patient care. By accessing real-time patient information, nurses can quickly identify patients who require urgent attention and those who can wait, enabling them to allocate their time and resources effectively and improve patient outcomes.

Patient education is another area where CDSS can be beneficial. It provides nurses access to relevant educational materials and resources to share with patients and their families. This can enhance patients' understanding of their health conditions and treatment options so that they can make informed decisions about their care.

Nevertheless, nurses must be cautious about the limitations and ethical concerns associated with CDSS.[1] CDSS recommendations may not always align with individual patient preferences, raising ethical concerns regarding patient autonomy and decision-making. Furthermore, nurses must ensure the accuracy and quality of the data used by CDSS to avoid inaccurate recommendations and compromised patient safety.

CDSS is a valuable tool in nursing practice, providing timely information and guidance to improve patient care. Nurses must employ CDSS judiciously, recognize its limitations and potential ethical concerns, and apply its recommendations to individual patient needs and preferences.[9] Nurses can enhance their decision-making capabilities, promote patient safety, and deliver high-quality care by doing so.

Conclusion

In conclusion, CDSSs have become indispensable tools for healthcare providers to make informed decisions about patient care. While there may be challenges associated with CDSS implementation, the benefits are significant, and their adoption is crucial in delivering high-quality patient care. Nurses need to recognize the importance of CDSS and receive proper training to utilize it effectively in their practice. The potential of CDSS to improve patient outcomes and enhance the quality and efficiency of healthcare delivery is immense.

Over the years, CDSS has evolved and continues to grow in its potential impact on healthcare. With healthcare's increasing complexity and data-driven nature, CDSS empowers healthcare providers to stay updated with the latest clinical knowledge and assists them in delivering optimal patient care. Nurses can leverage CDSS to fulfill their roles as patient advocates, ensuring safe and effective care while promoting patient autonomy.

Moreover, CDSS plays a vital role in supporting evidence-based practice, which is essential for improving patient outcomes and ensuring patient safety. By integrating CDSS into clinical workflows, healthcare providers can access the latest evidence-based practices and clinical guidelines, reducing variations in decision-making and enhancing the quality of care. In addition to supporting patient care, CDSS also facilitates nursing research by providing access to large datasets that can be analyzed to identify patterns and relationships between variables. This enables nurses and other healthcare providers to gain new insights into patient care and identify areas for improvement.

As healthcare continues to advance, CDSS will increasingly influence clinical decision-making. Nurses must be prepared and competent in using CDSS effectively, continuously updating their knowledge about new developments in this rapidly evolving field. By doing so, nurses can ensure that CDSS is utilized to its full potential in providing high-quality patient care.

References

1. Sutton RT, Pincock D, Baumgart DC, Sadowski DC, Fedorak RN, Kroeker KI. An overview of clinical decision support systems: benefits, risks, and strategies for success. NPJ Digit Med. 2020;3:17. doi: 10.1038/s41746-020-0221-y. PMID: 32047862; PMCID: PMC7005290.

2. Berge GT, Granmo OC, Tveit TO, Munkvold, BE, Ruthjersen, AL, Sharma, J. Machine learning-driven clinical decision support system for concept-based searching: a field trial in a Norwegian hospital. BMC Med Inform Decision Making. 2023;23:5. https://doi.org/10.1186/s12911-023-02101-x.

3. Osheroff J, Teich, T, Levick, D, Saldana, L, Velasco, F, Sittig, F, Rogers, K, Jenders, R. *Improving Outcomes with Clinical Decision Support: An Implementer's Guide.* HIMSS Publishing, 2012.

4. Sim I, Gorman P, Greenes RA, Haynes RB, Kaplan B, Lehmann H, Tang PC. Clinical decision support systems for the practice of evidence-based medicine. J Am Med Inform Assoc. 2001;8(6):527–534. doi: 10.1136/jamia.2001.0080527. PMID: 11687560; PMCID: PMC130063.

5. Tcheng JE, Bakken S, Bates DW, Bonner III, H, Gandhi TK, Josephs M, Kawamoto K, Lomotan EA, Mackay E, Middleton B, Teich JM, Weingarten S, Lopez MH. *Optimizing strategies for clinical decision support: summary of a meeting series*, 2017. National Academy of Sciences. Retrieved from www.healthit.gov/sites/default/files/page/2018-04/Optimizing_Strategies_508.pdf.

6. The Evolution of Clinical Decision Support in Healthcare, 2021. Retrieved from https://hbr.org/sponsored/2021/03/the-evolution-of-clinical-decision-support-in-healthcare.

7. Chen Z, Liang N, Zhang H, Li H, Yang Y, Zong X, Chen Y, Wang Y, Shi N. Harnessing the power of clinical decision support systems: Challenges and opportunities. Open Heart. 2023;10(2):1–11. https://doi.org/10.1136/openhrt-2023-002432.

8. Wang L, Zhang Z, Wang D, Cao W, Zhou X, Zhang P, Liu J, Fan X, Tain F. Human-centered design and evaluation of AI-empowered clinical decision support systems: a systematic

review. Front. Comput. Sci. 2023;5:1–18. https://doi.org/
10.3389/fcomp.2023.1187299.

9. Evans E, Whicher D. What should oversight of clinical decision
support systems look like? AMA J Ethics. 2018;20(9):E857–E863.
https://doi.org/10.1001/amajethics.2018.857.

10. Alert Fatigue, 2019. Agency for Healthcare Research and
Quality. https://psnet.ahrq.gov/primer/alert-fatigue.

11. Meunier PY, Raynaud C, Guimaraes E, Gueyffier F, Letrilliart L.
Barriers and facilitators to the use of clinical decision support
systems in primary care: a mixed-methods systematic review.
Ann Family Med. 2023;21(1):57–69. https://doi.org/10.1370/
afm.2908>.

12. Adler S. How to secure patient information (PHI). The HIPAA
Journal. 2023. www.hipaajournal.com/secure-patient-informat
ion-phi/

13. Altynpara E. *Cybersecurity and data protection in healthcare*,
2022. Retrieved from www.forbes.com/sites/forbestechcouncil/
2022/02/15/cybersecurity-and-data-protection-in-healthcare/
?sh=14def6a35048.

14. Mebrahtu TF, Skyrme S, Randell R, Keenan AM, Bloor K,
Yang H, Andre D, Ledward A, King H, Thompson C. Effects
of computerised clinical decision support systems (CDSS)
on nursing and allied health professional performance and
patient outcomes: a systematic review of experimental and
observational studies. BMJ Open. 2021;11(12):e053886. https://
doi.org/10.1136/bmjopen-2021-053886.

15. Patkar V. *Future trends in clinical decision support systems
(CDSS)*, 2022. Retrieved from https://healthcaretransformers.
com/digital-health/current-trends/clinical-decision-support-syst
ems-cdss/.

16. White NM, Carter HE, Kularatna S, Borg DN, Brain DC, Tariq
A, Abell B, Blythe R, McPhail SM. Evaluating the costs and
consequences of computerized clinical decision support
systems in hospitals: a scoping review and recommendations
for future practice. J Am Med Inform Assoc. 2023;30(6):1205–
1218. https://doi.org/10.1093/jamia/ocad040.

17. Jacob V, Thota AB, Chattopadhyay SK, Njie GJ, Proia KK,
Hopkins DP, Ross MN, Pronk NP, Clymer JM. Cost and
economic benefit of clinical decision support systems for

cardiovascular disease prevention: a community guide systematic review. J Am Med Inform Assoc. 2017;24(3):669–676. https://doi.org/10.1093/jamia/ocw160.

18. Donovan T, Abell B, Fernando M, McPhail SM, Carter HE. Implementation costs of hospital-based computerised decision support systems: a systematic review. Implement Sci. 2023;18(1):7. https://doi.org/10.1186/s13012-023-01261-8.

Chapter 5

Artificial Intelligence

Introduction to Artificial Intelligence in Nursing Informatics

Artificial intelligence (AI) is a branch of computer science that focuses on developing intelligent machines capable of performing tasks that typically require human intelligence.[1] In healthcare and nursing informatics, AI is the application of intelligent systems and algorithms to improve healthcare delivery, decision-making, and patient outcomes. AI is highly relevant to healthcare and nursing informatics due to its potential to transform healthcare delivery and management. With the exponential growth of digital data and technological advancements, AI can effectively process and analyze vast amounts of healthcare data, generating actionable insights and supporting evidence-based care. The growing importance of AI in healthcare delivery and decision-making stems from its ability to assist healthcare providers in various ways. AI algorithms can analyze complex medical data, including

   DOI: 10.4324/9781003439721-5

electronic health records (EHRs), medical images, and genomic information, to identify patterns, predict outcomes, and assist in diagnosis and treatment planning. AI-powered clinical decision support system (CDSS) provides real-time recommendations and alerts, enabling healthcare providers to make well-informed decisions at the point of care.

Nurse informaticists are crucial in leveraging AI technologies to enhance nursing practice and patient care. As experts in healthcare information technology, data management, and clinical workflows, nurse informaticists are well-positioned to drive the adoption and integration of AI solutions in healthcare settings. They possess the knowledge and skills to understand nursing practice's unique needs and challenges and can work collaboratively with interdisciplinary teams to implement AI tools effectively. Nurse informaticists contribute to AI initiatives by liaising between healthcare providers and technology developers, ensuring that AI solutions align with nursing workflows and clinical requirements. They provide critical insights into the design and customization of AI systems to enhance usability and maximize their impact on nursing practice. Moreover, nurse informaticists play a vital role in data governance and management, ensuring the quality, integrity, and security of healthcare data used in AI applications. They collaborate with data scientists and information technology specialists to develop robust data infrastructure, standards, and protocols for collecting, storing, and sharing data, ensuring that AI algorithms are trained on reliable and representative datasets.

Additionally, nurse informaticists contribute to AI's ethical and responsible use in nursing informatics. They navigate the ethical considerations of privacy, consent, bias, and transparency, ensuring that AI systems prioritize patient safety, autonomy, and equitable care. Nurse informaticists can actively engage in discussions on ethical guidelines, governance frameworks, and regulatory compliance to address the potential risks and challenges associated with AI implementation. The introduction to AI in healthcare and its relevance to nursing informatics emphasize its growing importance in healthcare delivery and decision-making. It highlights the specific role of nurse informaticists in leveraging AI technologies, including their expertise in driving AI adoption, ensuring data governance, and navigating ethical considerations. By harnessing AI capabilities, nurse informaticists contribute to improving clinical practice, patient care, and healthcare outcomes.

Fundamentals of AI

AI is based on the idea of creating intelligent systems that can mimic human intelligence and perform tasks that require human-like cognitive abilities.[1] Through advanced algorithms, machine learning, and other AI techniques, computer systems can analyze data, learn from patterns, and make informed decisions or provide accurate translations. By harnessing AI capabilities, machines can process and understand information in ways that resemble human cognitive abilities, enabling them to assist humans in many tasks and enhance overall efficiency and effectiveness in various domains.

AI in nursing informatics refers to using computer-based algorithms and machine-learning techniques to analyze and interpret large amounts of patient data.[2] It uses advanced technologies, such as natural language processing (NLP), predictive analytics, and deep learning, to automate and enhance clinical decision-making and care management.

AI in nursing informatics represents a paradigm shift in how healthcare data is analyzed and interpreted. By leveraging the power of machine learning algorithms and predictive analytics, AI can help healthcare providers make better-informed decisions about patient care, leading to improved patient outcomes and enhanced efficiency in healthcare delivery.

Types of AI in Nursing Informatics

The various types of AI in nursing informatics make significant contributions to enhancing healthcare delivery, streamlining workflows, supporting clinical decision-making, and facilitating nurses' daily practice. These AI technologies empower nurses with valuable tools and resources and have the potential to revolutionize nursing practice, improve patient outcomes, and streamline workflows.

Leveraging AI in nursing informatics enhances healthcare delivery through increased efficiency and accuracy. AI-powered systems can automate routine tasks, such as data entry and documentation, enabling nurses to allocate more time to direct patient care. Additionally, AI-based CDSS assists nurses in making informed decisions by providing real-time, evidence-based recommendations and alerts, ultimately improving patient safety and outcomes.

CDSS is one of the prominent applications of AI in nursing informatics. AI-powered CDSS uses algorithms to analyze patient data, medical literature, and clinical guidelines to provide healthcare providers with evidence-based alerts, notifications, and recommendations. These systems assist healthcare providers in making informed decisions at the point of care, enhancing diagnostic accuracy, treatment selection, and patient safety. For instance, AI algorithms can analyze patient symptoms, laboratory results, and medical history to support healthcare providers in diagnosing conditions, identifying potential risks, and suggesting appropriate treatment plans.

AI technologies also play a vital role in streamlining workflows. By automating processes, AI systems reduce administrative burdens, enhance care coordination, and promote efficient information exchange among healthcare teams. This streamlined workflow enables nurses to focus more on direct patient care, fostering improved patient satisfaction and quality of care. Furthermore, AI supports nurses in clinical decision-making by analyzing large volumes of patient data, identifying patterns, and predicting potential risks or outcomes. This assists nurses in identifying early warning signs, preventing adverse events, and tailoring treatment plans to individual patient needs. AI-powered predictive analytics can also aid nurses in identifying patients at high risk for specific conditions or re-admissions, allowing for proactive interventions and improved care management.

Patient monitoring is another crucial area in which AI makes significant contributions. AI-powered monitoring systems continuously collect and analyze patient data in real time, detecting patterns, anomalies, and changes in health status.[3] These systems enable early detection of deterioration, allowing nurses to intervene promptly and prevent adverse events. For example, AI algorithms can analyze vital signs, respiratory patterns, and trends in patient data to identify early signs of sepsis or other critical conditions, enabling nurses to initiate timely interventions.

AI also plays a crucial role in data analysis, supporting nurses in extracting valuable insights from vast amounts of healthcare data. AI algorithms can analyze structured and unstructured data, such as electronic health records, medical images, and research articles, to identify patterns, trends, and correlations.[4] This aids nurses in research, quality improvement initiatives, and evidence-based practice. For instance, AI can assist in analyzing patient data to identify factors contributing to medication errors, hospital re-admissions, or the effectiveness of specific interventions.

Telehealth is another area where AI has transformative potential in nursing informatics. AI technologies can support remote patient monitoring, virtual consultations, and personalized patient engagement. Virtual assistants, powered by AI, can deliver personalized patient education materials, answer patient queries, and support self-care management.[5] This promotes patient engagement and empowers individuals to participate in their care actively.

Specific examples and case studies demonstrate successful AI implementations in nursing informatics. Another example is the use of AI-powered NLP to extract and analyze patient data from clinical narratives, enabling nurses to identify adverse drug events and improve medication safety (Table 5.1).[6]

Table 5.1   Types of Artificial Intelligence in Healthcare

Machine learning (ML)	Machine learning algorithms are utilized to analyze large amounts of data and identify patterns, relationships, and anomalies. ML can be applied to tasks such as disease diagnosis, treatment planning, patient monitoring, and prediction of outcomes. ML algorithms learn from data and improve their performance over time, making them valuable in areas like medical imaging, genomics, and personalized medicine.
Natural language processing (NLP)	NLP involves the ability of computer systems to understand and interpret human language. In healthcare, NLP is used for tasks such as speech recognition, clinical documentation, and information extraction from medical records. NLP enables the conversion of unstructured data (such as physician's notes) into structured information, facilitating analysis and decision-making.

(continued)

Table 5.1 (Continued)

Large language models (LLMs)	LLMs refer to a sophisticated AI system designed to understand and generate human-like language. It is trained on vast amounts of textual data, enabling it to comprehend, generate, and respond to written or spoken language in a coherent and contextually appropriate manner.
Computer vision	Computer vision technologies are employed to analyze visual data, such as medical images and videos. In healthcare, computer vision is used for tasks like radiology image analysis, pathology slide interpretation, and surgical guidance. Computer vision algorithms can detect abnormalities, segment organs or tissues, and assist in diagnostic and therapeutic procedures.
Rule-based expert systems	Expert systems are AI-based systems that mimic the decision-making processes of human experts in specific domains. In healthcare, expert systems are utilized for clinical decision support, offering recommendations based on patient data, medical guidelines, and research evidence. Expert systems can aid in diagnosis, treatment selection, and medication management.
Robotics	Robotics involves the use of physical robots or robotic systems to perform tasks autonomously or with human guidance. In healthcare, robotics finds applications in surgery, rehabilitation, and patient assistance. Robotic surgical systems enable precise and minimally invasive procedures, while assistive robots can help with activities of daily living and support patient monitoring.
Virtual assistants	Virtual assistants, powered by AI, are conversational agents that can interact with users and provide information or perform tasks. In healthcare, virtual assistants can assist with appointment scheduling, answer patient inquiries, provide health information, and offer personalized recommendations. Virtual assistants can enhance patient engagement and support healthcare professionals in delivering care.

Source: Davenport T, Kalakota R. The potential for artificial intelligence in healthcare. Future Healthcare J. 2019;6(2):94–98. doi: 10.7861/futurehosp.6-2-94. PMID: 31363513; PMCID: PMC6616181.

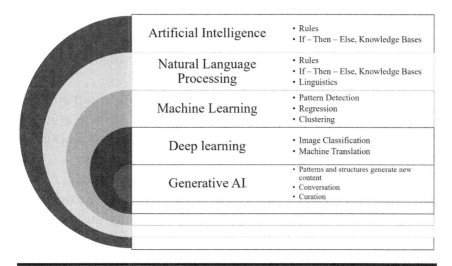

Artificial Intelligence	• Rules • If – Then – Else, Knowledge Bases
Natural Language Processing	• Rules • If – Then – Else, Knowledge Bases • Linguistics
Machine Learning	• Pattern Detection • Regression • Clustering
Deep learning	• Image Classification • Machine Translation
Generative AI	• Patterns and structures generate new content • Conversation • Curation

Figure 5.1 Artificial intelligence operations. (Modified from *Nursing informatics: Scope and standards of practice* (3rd ed.). (2022). American Nurses Association.)

AI applications in nursing informatics are diverse and impactful. AI assists with clinical decision support, patient monitoring, data analysis, and telehealth, among other things. It enhances nursing practice, improves patient outcomes, and streamlines workflows. Integrating AI in nursing informatics benefits healthcare delivery by improving clinical decision-making, optimizing workflows, and supporting nurses in their daily practice (Figure 5.1).

Ethical and Legal Considerations

AI is becoming more prevalent in healthcare, and it is essential to consider the ethical and legal aspects of AI in nursing informatics, such as privacy, data security, bias, and transparency. It also highlights the need for ethical standards and regulatory frameworks to ensure responsible and ethical AI implementation. The collection and analysis of patient data for AI algorithms must adhere to strict privacy regulations to safeguard sensitive health information.[7]

Data security is another critical aspect of AI in nursing informatics. AI systems rely on vast amounts of data, and the secure handling and storage of the data are paramount. Nurse informaticists must verify that robust security measures are implemented to protect data against data breaches, unauthorized access, and cyber threats. Ensuring encryption, access controls, and regular security audits are essential to maintaining the integrity and confidentiality of patient data.

Bias in AI algorithms is a significant concern that can impact patient care. AI algorithms are trained on data that may contain biases and disparities. If not addressed, these biases can perpetuate existing healthcare disparities and inequities. Nurse informaticists must actively address bias in AI algorithms by carefully selecting and curating diverse and representative datasets, ensuring fairness, and regularly monitoring and evaluating algorithm performance.

Transparency in AI algorithms is crucial to understanding how decisions are made. Nurse informaticists should ensure AI systems are transparent and explainable, enabling healthcare providers to understand the reasoning behind AI-generated recommendations. Transparency fosters trust in AI systems and allows healthcare providers to validate the accuracy and reliability of AI-generated insights.[8]

The development and implementation of ethical guidelines and regulatory frameworks are essential to guide AI's responsible and ethical use in nursing informatics. Professional nursing organizations, regulatory bodies, and government entities play a crucial role in establishing standards and guidelines for AI implementation. These guidelines address informed consent, data protection, fairness, accountability, and transparency. Nurse informaticists should familiarize themselves with these guidelines and incorporate them into their AI projects to ensure ethical practice.

Regulatory frameworks, such as data protection regulations and healthcare legislation, also shape AI's ethical and legal landscape in nursing informatics. Compliance with HIPAA and the General Data Protection Regulation (GDPR)[8] are essential to protecting patient privacy and maintaining the legal integrity of AI implementations. Moreover, interdisciplinary collaborations involving nurses, informaticists, ethicists, policymakers, and legal experts are essential for addressing ethical and legal considerations in AI implementation. These collaborations foster discussions, knowledge sharing, and the development of comprehensive frameworks[8] that balance innovation with patient rights and ethical principles.

In summary, AI implementation in nursing informatics requires careful consideration of ethical and legal implications. Privacy, data security, bias, and transparency are vital concerns that must be addressed to ensure responsible and ethical AI practice. Developing and adhering to ethical guidelines and regulatory frameworks are vital for guiding AI implementation. By prioritizing patient privacy, data security, fairness, and transparency, nurses and informaticists can navigate the ethical and legal complexities associated with AI and contribute to the advancement of AI in nursing informatics.

Challenges and Barriers

The practical implementation of AI in healthcare faces various challenges and barriers. This section identifies these challenges and discusses data quality, interoperability, resistance to change, and resource constraints. It also provides strategies and recommendations for overcoming these challenges.

Data quality and integrity are critical issues in AI implementation. The quality, completeness, and reliability of healthcare data influence how well AI algorithms work and produce results. Incomplete or erroneous data can lead to biased results and compromised patient care. Nurses and informaticists must ensure data quality by implementing data validation processes, ensuring data integrity, and collaborating with data stewards to improve data accuracy and completeness. Interoperability is another critical challenge in AI implementation. Healthcare systems often use disparate data sources and EHR systems that do not communicate with each other. This lack of interoperability hinders integrating and exchanging data necessary for AI applications. Nurses and informaticists should advocate for standardized data formats, standard data models, and health information exchange (HIE) protocols to facilitate interoperability and enable AI-driven insights across healthcare systems.

Resistance to change poses a significant barrier to AI implementation. Healthcare professionals may be hesitant to embrace AI technologies due to fear of job displacement, lack of familiarity, or concerns about the reliability of AI-generated recommendations. To address this, nurses and informaticists should engage in comprehensive change management strategies, including education and training programs, to promote a positive AI culture. Demonstrating the benefits and value of AI, involving stakeholders in the decision-making process, and fostering collaboration and communication are essential for overcoming resistance to change.

Resource constraints, including financial limitations and limited technological infrastructure, can impede the implementation of AI in nursing informatics. AI initiatives often require substantial technological investments, data storage, computational resources, and skilled personnel. Nurses and informaticists should actively advocate for resource allocation and seek collaborations with stakeholders to secure necessary funding and support. Exploring partnerships with technology vendors, research institutions, and governmental agencies can help alleviate resource constraints and promote successful AI implementation.

Several strategies and recommendations can be utilized to overcome these challenges and barriers. The strategy of fostering collaboration and partnerships is a powerful approach to overcoming challenges and barriers in the context of AI solutions. Interdisciplinary collaborations involve bringing together professionals from various fields, such as nursing, informatics, technology development, research, and policymaking. Each field brings a unique perspective and set of skills that contribute to developing and implementing AI solutions. For instance, nurses provide insights into patient care needs and workflows, informaticists guide the design and integration of AI technologies into existing systems, technology developers create the actual AI tools, researchers evaluate the effectiveness of these tools, and policymakers ensure that the use of AI in healthcare is ethical and equitable.

Partnerships among different stakeholders facilitate the sharing of resources and knowledge, accelerating the development and adoption of AI solutions.[9] These partnerships could be between different healthcare organizations, between healthcare organizations and technology companies, or between public and private entities. For example, a partnership between a healthcare organization and a technology company could result in the development of an AI tool tailored to the specific needs of that organization. The collaboration and partnerships strategy is about bringing different professionals together and effectively leveraging diverse perspectives and expertise. This requires creating an environment where all voices are heard and valued, and collaborative decision-making is the norm. It also involves ongoing education and training to ensure that all team members understand AI and its potential impact on healthcare. These collaborations and partnerships aim to address challenges and develop effective AI solutions. This could involve identifying and addressing technical issues, such as data quality and algorithm bias, as well as non-technical issues, such as ethical considerations and workforce impacts. It could also involve developing strategies for evaluating AI solutions' effectiveness and scaling up successful solutions.

Fostering collaboration and partnerships is a powerful strategy for overcoming the challenges associated with AI in healthcare. It allows for pooling resources and expertise, facilitates knowledge sharing, and promotes the development of effective and equitable AI solutions. However, careful planning and management are required to ensure that all voices are heard and that collaborations and partnerships are productive and sustainable.

The strategy of comprehensive education and training programs for nurses and healthcare professionals is crucial in enhancing their understanding of AI concepts, benefits, and limitations. These programs should be designed to cover a wide range of AI topics, from the basics of AI and machine learning to more advanced concepts such as deep learning and NLP. In addition to theoretical knowledge, these programs should also focus on the practical applications of AI in healthcare. This includes predictive analytics, medical imaging, genomics, and patient management. By gaining hands-on experience with AI tools and technologies, healthcare professionals can better understand how to utilize them in their practice effectively.[10] It is not just about understanding how AI works. It is equally essential for healthcare professionals to understand AI's potential benefits and limitations. For instance, while AI can significantly aid in diagnosing diseases and predicting patient outcomes, it is also essential to recognize that AI models are only as good as the data they are trained on. These models may perform differently than expected if presented with significantly different data from their training data. The curriculum should also address the ethical considerations of using AI in healthcare. This includes issues related to patient privacy, data security, and the implications of AI decisions on patient care. Given the rapid evolution of AI, continuing education programs should be in place to ensure that healthcare professionals stay updated with the latest developments. This will enable them to effectively utilize AI technologies and embrace their potential to improve patient care and outcomes.

Data governance plays a pivotal role in successfully implementing and utilizing AI technologies. It involves establishing robust frameworks that ensure data quality, integrity, and security. Quality improvement initiatives in the data used for AI algorithms begin with ensuring the quality of the data. This involves checking for accuracy, consistency, and completeness in the data. High-quality data is essential for training reliable AI models, as poor-quality data can lead to inaccurate predictions and insights. A crucial step in quality improvement is data cleaning, which involves identifying and correcting errors in the data, such as inconsistencies, duplicates, and missing values. This process can significantly improve the performance of AI algorithms. Another important aspect is data standardization, which means transforming data into a standard format. This makes it easier for AI algorithms to process and analyze the data. Standardization can involve scaling numerical data, encoding categorical data, and handling missing values. Data validation processes are used to verify the accuracy of the data. This can involve cross-checking the data with other sources, using statistical methods to detect anomalies, and reviewing the data manually. Quality improvement is an ongoing process. It involves continuously monitoring the AI algorithms' data and performance, identifying improvement areas, and implementing changes as needed. This continuous improvement ensures the reliability and effectiveness of AI algorithms in various applications.

Developing change management strategies in healthcare, particularly with the integration of AI, involves several key components. Clear communication ensures that all stakeholders, including nurses and other healthcare professionals, understand the implemented changes and their reasons. This involves conveying the technical aspects of AI and emphasizing its role in enhancing patient care outcomes.[10] Stakeholder engagement is another critical aspect of successful change management. This means involving healthcare professionals in decision-making, ensuring their voices are heard and their concerns are addressed. Buy-in from these professionals is essential for successfully implementing AI technologies in healthcare settings. The role of AI in enhancing patient care outcomes should be emphasized throughout this process. AI can potentially improve disease diagnosis, treatment selection, and patient monitoring, enabling more accurate and efficient healthcare delivery.[10] However, addressing any concerns healthcare professionals may have about AI is also important. This can be done through open dialogue and continuous support. Concerns may include data privacy, bias, and the need for human expertise.[10] Addressing concerns, providing clear explanations, and offering continuous support can help alleviate these concerns and foster a more accepting and positive attitude towards AI. Developing effective change management strategies for implementing AI in healthcare requires clear communication, stakeholder engagement, emphasis on the benefits of AI, and addressing concerns through open dialogue and continuous support.

Supporting the development and implementation of ethical AI practices, data privacy, and interoperability is essential in the present technological environment. Ethical AI practices involve ensuring fairness, transparency, and accountability in AI systems.[11] Healthcare organizations need a clear plan to deal with potential ethical quandaries that AI technologies may introduce. This includes identifying existing infrastructure that an AI ethics program can leverage, creating a data and AI ethical risk framework tailored to the industry, and building organizational awareness. Protecting data privacy in an AI-driven world is a significant concern. AI technologies can potentially infringe upon the fundamental rights of individuals if not managed according to clear principles and practices. Good data hygiene, using accurate, fair, and representative data sets, and limiting data exploitation are some ways to protect privacy in AI.

Interoperability, the ability of two systems to communicate effectively, is a critical factor in the future of machine learning. It allows many different models to come together, which is essential for the healthcare industry. Interoperability in AI can enhance our lives by allowing for more robust, faster translation between information platforms.

Staying informed about evolving regulations and guidelines is essential to ensure compliance and alignment with best practices. The AI regulatory landscape is quickly shifting, with various countries and organizations working on developing policies and guidelines to address the challenges posed by AI technologies. Advocating for ethical AI practices, data privacy, interoperability, and staying informed about evolving regulations and guidelines are crucial steps towards ensuring the responsible and beneficial use of AI technologies. These practices help align with the best practices and play a significant role in shaping the future of AI.

Another strategy is to initiate AI implementation with pilot projects and small-scale initiatives to demonstrate value and build confidence. These smaller projects serve as a platform to demonstrate AI's value, thereby building stakeholder confidence. Once these initial projects succeed, the next step is gradually scaling up the implementations. This scaling process should be carried out in a controlled and measured manner, ensuring that the growth of AI usage aligns with the organization's capacity and readiness. Throughout this process, continuous evaluation and refinement of AI systems are crucial. Feedback from users and outcomes from the AI systems should be used to make necessary adjustments and improvements. This iterative process of evaluation and refinement ensures that the AI systems remain effective and continue to deliver value as they are scaled up.

Nurses and informaticists can overcome barriers to AI implementation in nursing informatics by addressing these challenges and implementing these strategies. This paves the way for successfully integrating AI technologies, ultimately improving patient care, enhancing workflow efficiency, and driving positive healthcare outcomes.

Future Directions and Opportunities

AI in nursing informatics is poised for significant advancements. Some emerging trends include the development of more sophisticated machine learning algorithms, such as deep learning and reinforcement learning. These advanced techniques hold promise for handling complex healthcare data and improving the accuracy and efficiency of AI applications.

Another trend is the evolution of AI algorithms for predictive analytics and precision medicine. These algorithms enable more precise predictions, risk assessments, and personalized treatment plans. By analyzing diverse patient data, including genomics, lifestyle factors, and environmental influences, AI can support nurses in delivering precision medicine tailored to individual patient needs.

NLP techniques are also advancing, enabling AI systems to understand and generate more contextually relevant and accurate responses. This will enhance clinical documentation, support conversational AI interfaces, and enable seamless interactions between nurses and AI-powered systems.

Large language models (LLMs) are another emerging trend. Chatbots that use these models can communicate naturally with patients, nurses, and others, providing them with information, advice, and help. LLMs can also condense medical documents and help nurses identify care plans.[12] Moreover, they can streamline documentation, coding, billing, and reporting, increasing efficiency and accuracy for nurses. Additionally, LLMs can enhance nurse education and training by generating customized and flexible learning materials, quizzes, and feedback. AI is rapidly evolving, and its potential impact on nursing informatics is immense. AI's emerging trends and future directions in nursing informatics present numerous opportunities for nurse informaticists to contribute to AI research, development, and implementation.

Advanced AI technologies like robotics, virtual reality (VR), augmented reality (AR), and mixed reality (MR) can have a profound impact on nursing informatics. Robotics and automation technologies, including robotic process automation (RPA) and robotic assistants, have the potential to streamline workflows, assist with repetitive tasks, and enhance patient care delivery.[13] They can alleviate the physical demands of nurses and improve patient safety. These technologies have the potential to streamline workflows, assist with repetitive tasks, and enhance patient care delivery. For instance, RPA can handle administrative tasks like scheduling and billing, freeing nurses to focus more on patient care. On the other hand, robotic assistants can help with tasks like lifting patients or delivering supplies, thereby alleviating the physical demands on nurses.[14] These technologies not only improve efficiency but also enhance patient safety.

Nurse informaticists play a crucial role in the successful implementation of these technologies. They can contribute by evaluating robotic systems' usability, safety, and effectiveness. This involves assessing whether the technology meets its intended goals, operates safely in the healthcare environment, and improves outcomes. Nurse informaticists can ensure the seamless integration of these technologies with nursing workflows. This means ensuring that technology fits smoothly into nurses' existing processes and routines rather than disrupting them. It also means providing training and support to nurses as they adapt to the new technology.

Robotics and automation technologies hold immense potential for nursing informatics. These technologies can transform nursing practice by streamlining workflows, assisting with repetitive tasks, and enhancing patient care delivery. With their unique blend of clinical and technical expertise, nurse informaticists are ideally positioned to lead this transformation.

Virtual reality (VR) can create immersive simulated environments that allow nurses to practice skills, conduct virtual patient assessments, and enhance training.[15,16] It offers opportunities for realistic simulation, collaborative learning, and remote education. Realistic simulations can mimic real-world clinical scenarios, helping nurses to develop critical thinking and decision-making skills. Collaborative learning allows nurses to work together in the virtual environment, promoting teamwork and communication skills. Remote education enables nurses to access VR training programs anywhere, making education more accessible and flexible.

Nurse informaticists play a crucial role in designing and implementing VR-based training programs. They can explore different VR technologies, design immersive and interactive VR scenarios, and ensure that the VR training programs align with the learning objectives of the nursing curriculum. Nurse informaticists can evaluate the effectiveness of VR training programs in improving nursing competency and performance. This involves assessing whether the VR training improves nurses' knowledge, skills, and attitudes and whether it translates into improved patient care in the real world.[16] In conclusion, VR is a powerful tool in nursing informatics, offering immense potential for enhancing nursing education and training. By creating immersive simulated environments, promoting realistic simulation and collaborative learning, and enabling remote education, VR can transform how nurses are trained and prepared for the real world.

Augmented reality (AR) is a groundbreaking technology that overlays digital information onto the real-world environment, significantly enhancing situational awareness and decision-making.[17,18] AR can assist nurses in many ways. For instance, it can provide real-time patient data, which can be crucial in monitoring patient health and making timely decisions. AR can also visualize anatomical structures, aiding nurses in understanding complex medical conditions and planning appropriate care. AR can guide procedures, ensuring accuracy and safety.

Nurse informaticists play a pivotal role in successfully integrating AR into healthcare. They can contribute by exploring AR applications that enhance clinical workflows, improving efficiency and patient care. They can also evaluate

the safety of AR applications, ensuring that they do not
pose any risks to patients or healthcare providers. Nurse
informaticists can optimize care delivery by identifying ways
AR can improve patient outcomes. AR is a powerful tool in
nursing informatics, offering immense potential for enhancing
patient care, improving medical practices, and revolutionizing
healthcare delivery.

Mixed reality (MR) is a transformative technological
paradigm in healthcare, revolutionizing patient care and
medical practices by merging the physical and digital realms.[19]
MR offers healthcare professionals immersive and interactive
experiences by seamlessly blending virtual elements with the
real world. These experiences enhance various aspects of
healthcare, including medical training, diagnosis, treatment,
and patient education.[15] MR can facilitate medical procedures,
making them simpler and safer for patients. It includes
applications such as surgical simulation, robot training, and
expert training. MR can also provide healthcare professionals
with 3D objects displayed in their environment, allowing them
to interact with these objects. This interaction enhances their
understanding and improves their ability to diagnose and treat
patients. MR can revolutionize medical training by providing
realistic, immersive simulations. These simulations allow
healthcare professionals to practice skills and conduct virtual
patient assessments in a safe and controlled environment. MR
is a powerful tool in healthcare, offering immense potential
to enhance patient care, improve medical practices, and
revolutionize healthcare delivery.

Nurse informaticists have a vital role in making MR work
well in healthcare. They can help by finding MR applications
that improve clinical processes, making them more efficient
and patient-centered. They can also assess MR applications'
safety, ensuring they do not harm patients or healthcare
providers. Nurse informaticists can enhance care quality

by finding ways MR can benefit patient outcomes. MR is a valuable tool in nursing informatics, offering great possibilities for improving patient care, advancing medical practices, and transforming healthcare delivery.

Opportunities for Nurse Informaticists

Nurse informaticists can make valuable contributions to AI research, development, and implementation. They can conduct research that examines the effectiveness, usability, and ethical issues of AI applications in nursing practice. They can do studies to assess the effect of AI on patient outcomes, workflow efficiency, and nursing performance. Nurse informaticists can work with technologists, data scientists, and researchers to create AI-driven solutions tailored to nursing practice. Nurse informaticists can help develop AI technologies that match nursing values and priorities by promoting interdisciplinary collaboration.

Nurse informaticists can lead the education and training of nurses and healthcare professionals about AI concepts, applications, and ethics. They can create curricula, workshops, and training programs to improve AI literacy among nursing professionals. Nurse informaticists can influence AI policy and governance frameworks by supporting ethical standards, privacy protections, and regulations that encourage responsible AI use in nursing informatics. They can join professional organizations and contribute to discussions and initiatives related to AI ethics and regulations.

Nurse informaticists can play an essential role in shaping the future of AI in healthcare by following emerging trends, using advanced AI technologies, and taking advantage of opportunities. Their expertise in nursing practice, informatics, and technology enables them to lead the responsible and effective implementation of AI, ultimately improving patient care outcomes and transforming healthcare delivery.

Conclusion

In conclusion, AI is a branch of computer science that develops intelligent machines that can perform tasks that typically require human intelligence. AI is highly relevant to nursing informatics, as it can improve patient outcomes, enhance care quality, and increase healthcare delivery efficiency. AI applications in nursing are diverse and impactful. AI can assist with clinical decision support, patient monitoring, data analysis, telehealth, and more. AI can also leverage advanced techniques like NLP, predictive analytics, and deep learning to process and understand complex healthcare data.

AI implementation requires careful consideration of ethical and legal implications, such as privacy, data security, bias, and transparency. Nurse informaticists play a vital role in ensuring AI's ethical and responsible use by adhering to ethical guidelines, regulatory frameworks, and data governance standards. They also collaborate with other stakeholders to address AI's potential risks and challenges.

The practical implementation of AI in healthcare faces various challenges and barriers, such as data quality, interoperability, resistance to change, and resource constraints. Nurse informaticists can overcome these challenges by implementing data validation processes, advocating for standardized data formats, engaging in comprehensive change management strategies, and seeking collaborations and partnerships with other stakeholders.

AI in nursing informatics is poised for significant advancements, with emerging trends such as more sophisticated machine learning algorithms, precision medicine, LLM, and MR. These technologies hold promise for enhancing nursing practice, education, and research. Nurse informaticists can make valuable contributions to AI research, development, and implementation by conducting research, educating and training nurses, influencing AI policy and governance, and leading the integration of AI technologies into healthcare settings.

AI is revolutionizing nursing informatics by leveraging advanced data analytics and machine learning techniques to empower healthcare providers to make more informed decisions about patient care. With applications ranging from clinical decision support to patient monitoring, disease diagnosis and management, and personalized medicine, AI has the potential to significantly improve patient outcomes and enhance the overall quality of care provided. By automating complex processes, providing real-time insights, and identifying patterns in patient data, AI enables healthcare providers to deliver more accurate and personalized care. As AI technology advances, it holds immense potential to transform healthcare delivery and drive positive changes in nursing informatics.

References

1. Pan Y. Heading toward artificial intelligence 2.0. Engineering. 2016;2(4):409–413.
2. McGrow K. Artificial intelligence: essentials for nursing. Nursing. 2019;49(9):46–49. doi: 10.1097/01.NURSE.

0000577716.57052.8d. PMID: 31365455; PMCID: PMC6716553.

3. Feng J, Phillips RV, Malenica I, Bishara A, Hubbard AE, Celi LA, Pirracchio R. Clinical artificial intelligence quality improvement: towards continual monitoring and updating of AI algorithms in healthcare. NPJ Digit Med. 2022;5(1):66. doi: 10.1038/s41746-022-00611-y. PMID: 35641814; PMCID: PMC9156743.

4. Bohr A, Memarzadeh K. The rise of artificial intelligence in healthcare applications. Artificial Intel Healthcare. 2020;1:25–60. doi: 10.1016/B978-0-12-818438-7.00002-2. Epub June 26, 2020. PMCID: PMC7325854.

5. Jadczyk T, Wojakowski W, Tendera M, Henry TD, Egnaczyk G, Shreenivas S. Artificial intelligence can improve patient management at the time of a pandemic: the role of voice technology. J Med Internet Res. 2021;23(5):e22959. doi: 10.2196/22959. PMID: 33999834; PMCID: PMC8153030.

6. Yang X, Chen A, PourNejatian N, Shin HC, Smith KE, Parisien C, Compas C, Martin C, Costa AB, Flores MG, Zhang Y, Magoc T, Harle CA, Lipori G, Mitchell DA, Hogan WR, Shenkman EA, Bian J, Wu Y. A large language model for electronic health records. NPJ Digit Med. 2022;5(1):194. doi: 10.1038/s41746-022-00742-2. PMID: 36572766; PMCID: PMC9792464.

7. Murdoch B. Privacy and artificial intelligence: challenges for protecting health information in a new era. BMC Med Ethics. 2021;22:122. https://doi.org/10.1186/s12910-021-00687-3.

8. Kiseleva A, Kotzinos D, de Hert P. Transparency of AI in healthcare as a multilayered system of accountabilities: between legal requirements and technical limitations. Front Artificial Intel. 2022;5. https://doi.org/10.3389/frai.2022.879603.

9. Kaiser L, Bartz S, Neugebauer EAM, Pietsch B, Pieper D. Interprofessional collaboration and patient-reported outcomes in inpatient care: protocol for a systematic review. System Rev. 2018;7(1):126. https://doi.org/10.1186/s13643-018-0797-3.

10. Alowais SA, Alghamdi SS, Alsuhebany N, Alqahtani T, Alshaya AI, Almohareb SN, Aldairem A, Alrashed M, bin Saleh K, Badreldin HA, al Yami MS, al Harbi S, Albekairy AM. Revolutionizing healthcare: the role of artificial intelligence in

clinical practice. BMC Med Edu. 2023;23(1):689. https://doi.org/10.1186/s12909-023-04698-z.

11. Gianni R, Lehtinen S, Nieminen M. Governance of responsible AI: from ethical guidelines to cooperative policies. Front Comput Sci. 2022;4:1–17. https://doi.org/10.3389/fcomp.2022.873437.

12. Nashwan AJ, Abujaber AA. Harnessing large language models in nursing care planning: opportunities, challenges, and ethical considerations. Cureus. 2023;15(6):e40542. doi: 10.7759/cureus.40542. PMID: 37465807; PMCID: PMC10350541.

13. Ribeiro J, Lima R, Eckhardt T, Paiva S. Robotic process automation artificial intelligence in industry 4.0 – a literature review. Procedia Comput Sci. 2021;181:51–58. https://doi.org/10.1016/j.procs.2021.01.104.

14. Ohneberg C, Stöbich N, Warmbein A, Rathgeber I, Mehler-Klamt AC, Fischer U, Eberl I. Assistive robotic systems in nursing care: a scoping review. BMC Nurs. 2023;22(1):72. https://doi.org/10.1186/s12912-023-01230-y.

15. Shah M. *Helpful resources for virtual reality simulations in nursing education*, n.d. Retrieved from https://evolve.elsevier.com/education/expertise/apply-clinical-judgment/virtual-reality-simulation-research-review-list/

16. Liu K, Zhang W, Li W, Wang T, Zheng Y. Effectiveness of virtual reality in nursing education: a systematic review and meta-analysis. BMC Med Edu. 2023;23(1):710. https://doi.org/10.1186/s12909-023-04662-x.

17. Marr B. *The important difference between augmented reality and mixed reality*. Forbes, July 19, 2019. https://bernardmarr.com/the-important-difference-between-virtual-reality-augmented-reality-and-mixed-reality/.

18. Gasteiger N, van der Veer SN, Wilson P, Dowding D. Upskilling health and care workers with augmented and virtual reality: protocol for a realist review to develop an evidence-informed programme theory. BMJ Open. 2021;11(7):e050033. https://doi.org/10.1136/bmjopen-2021-050033.

19. Kim KJ, Choi MJ, Kim KJ. Effects of nursing simulation using mixed reality: a scoping review. Healthcare. 2021;9(8):947. https://doi.org/10.3390/healthcare9080947.

Chapter 6

Telehealth and Telemedicine

History and Evolution of Telehealth and Telemedicine

Telehealth and telemedicine have been in use since the early 20th century. In 1906, the first telemedicine consultation was conducted between a hospital and a remote location in Pennsylvania using the telephone.[1] Over time, telemedicine has evolved from basic telephone consultations to the use of video conferencing, remote monitoring devices, and mobile health applications. The use of telehealth and telemedicine has increased significantly in recent years, with the COVID-19 pandemic driving a surge in its adoption. According to a report by the Centers for Disease Control and Prevention (CDC), the number of telehealth visits increased by 154% in the last week of March 2020 compared with the same period in 2019.[2]

 DOI: 10.4324/9781003439721-6

Over the years, telehealth and telemedicine have undergone significant technological advancements and policy changes. In the 1960s, NASA developed a telemedicine system that was used to monitor astronauts' vital signs during space missions. In the 1970s, telemedicine began to be used to provide medical care to patients in remote locations, such as rural areas or other remote locations.

The advent of the internet in the 1990s led to the development of web-based telemedicine applications, making it easier for healthcare providers to provide remote consultations and monitor patients from a distance. In 1996, the Health Insurance Portability and Accountability Act (HIPAA) was passed, which set standards for protecting patients' health information during telemedicine consultations.

In the early 2000s, mobile health (mHealth) applications began to emerge, enabling patients to monitor their health using smartphones and wearable devices. In 2010, the Affordable Care Act (ACA) was passed, which included provisions to expand the use of telemedicine in Medicare and Medicaid programs.

Telehealth and telemedicine are widely used to provide various medical services, including remote consultations, chronic disease management, mental health services, and emergency medical care. Telemedicine increased significantly during the COVID-19 pandemic as healthcare providers sought to provide safe and efficient care while minimizing the risk of infection exposure.

Telehealth and telemedicine are expected to continue to evolve and expand in the future with the integration of artificial intelligence (AI) and virtual reality (VR) technologies. These advancements have the potential to further enhance the quality and accessibility of healthcare services, particularly for patients in underserved or remote areas.

Benefits of Using Telehealth and Telemedicine

Telehealth and telemedicine offer several benefits, including improved access to healthcare, cost savings, and increased patient engagement.[3] Patients in remote or underserved areas can access healthcare services without traveling long distances, reducing the cost and time burden of receiving care. Telehealth and telemedicine can also reduce the need for in-person consultations, leading to cost savings for patients and healthcare providers.[4]

Telehealth and telemedicine can improve patient engagement by giving patients more control over their health and treatment. Patients can use telehealth and telemedicine to track their health, receive reminders about medication, and communicate with healthcare providers in real time, leading to better health outcomes. In addition to these benefits, telehealth and telemedicine can improve patient outcomes by facilitating earlier intervention and treatment. Patients can receive care and monitoring more frequently and conveniently, leading to faster identification and management of health issues. This can particularly benefit patients with chronic conditions or requiring frequent monitoring.

Telehealth and telemedicine can also improve healthcare provider efficiency and workflow. Healthcare providers can use telemedicine to see more patients in less time, reducing waiting times and improving patient satisfaction. It can also enable healthcare providers to work remotely, improving work–life balance and increasing job satisfaction.[5]

Furthermore, telehealth and telemedicine can play a significant role in public health emergencies, such as the COVID-19 pandemic. Telemedicine enables healthcare providers to triage and manage patients remotely, reducing the risk of infection transmission while ensuring patients receive timely care. Telehealth and telemedicine offer several benefits to patients and healthcare providers, including improved access to care, cost savings, increased patient engagement, improved outcomes, and enhanced efficiency and workflow (Table 6.1).[3,4]

Table 6.1   Benefits of Telehealth

Benefit	Explanation
Enhanced ccess to healthcare	Telehealth and telemedicine eliminate distance limitations, enabling people in isolated or under-resourced areas to access healthcare services. This improved access is especially crucial for those who would otherwise have to travel far and pay a lot to see a healthcare provider. By closing this gap, telehealth and telemedicine ensure that people across different locations can receive medical care, thus advancing health equity.
Cost savings	Telehealth and telemedicine can offer significant cost benefits for both patients and healthcare providers. Patients can save money on travel-related expenses, such as transportation, accommodation, and lost work. Also, telehealth can take less time than in-person visits, allowing patients to keep their regular schedules. For healthcare providers, telemedicine can cut down on the costs of running physical clinics or hospitals. With fewer in-person consultations, there is less need for resources like examination rooms and staff time, which can reduce operational costs.
Increased patient engagement	With telehealth and telemedicine, patients have more control over their health and treatment. Patients can use digital tools to keep track of their conditions, get notifications for their medication, and talk to healthcare providers online. This way, patients can be more involved in managing their health, which helps them follow their treatment plans better and achieve better health results.

(continued)

Table 6.1 (Continued)

Benefit	Explanation
Early intervention and treatment	These technologies allow for faster and better management of health issues. Patients can get ongoing care and tracking, even at their homes, enabling the quick detection of possible health problems. This feature is particularly helpful for patients with long-term conditions or those who need regular monitoring. Early action can avoid the worsening of health issues, lowering the overall pressure on the healthcare system and enhancing patients' quality of life.
Healthcare provider efficiency	Telehealth can improve healthcare provider efficiency. By doing online consultations, healthcare professionals can treat more patients in less time, resulting in faster access to appointments and increased patient satisfaction. Furthermore, telemedicine helps healthcare providers to handle patient records more effectively, cutting down on paperwork and enabling a more attentive approach to patient care.
Work–life balance for healthcare providers	Telehealth and telemedicine provide healthcare providers with the flexibility to work remotely, offering a better work–life balance. This flexibility can lead to increased job satisfaction among healthcare professionals, reduce burnout rates, and potentially attract more talent to the healthcare industry.
Public health emergencies	Telemedicine is vital for dealing with public health emergencies like pandemics. In situations like the COVID-19 pandemic, telehealth enabled healthcare providers to assess and treat patients from a distance, reducing the chance of spreading infection while providing prompt and proper care for those involved. It serves as a valuable tool in maintaining continuity of care even in the face of crises.

Challenges of Using Telehealth and Telemedicine

While telehealth and telemedicine offer substantial benefits, they are not without their share of challenges, which must be addressed to ensure their widespread and equitable adoption in healthcare. The absence of comprehensive regulations and standards in the telehealth and telemedicine space can lead to inconsistent quality of care. The variability in licensing requirements across different regions can also hinder healthcare providers' ability to offer services across state or international borders. Establishing clear guidelines and regulations is essential to ensure patient safety and the effectiveness of these technologies.

Telehealth and telemedicine depend on reliable and secure internet connections. Unfortunately, not all patients have access to high-speed internet, especially in rural or underserved areas.[6] This digital divide can limit the reach of telehealth services and exacerbate healthcare disparities. Improving broadband infrastructure and expanding internet access are crucial to address this challenge. Healthcare providers must adapt to new technologies and workflows associated with telehealth and telemedicine. This includes proficiency in using telehealth platforms, effective communication via video conferencing, and the ability to provide high-quality remote care. Training and education programs are necessary to equip healthcare professionals with the skills to navigate this digital transformation effectively.

The reimbursement landscape for telehealth and telemedicine services can be complex and variable. Insurance companies may not uniformly cover these services, making them less affordable for some patients.[6] Additionally, healthcare providers may receive a different level of reimbursement for virtual visits than they do for in-person appointments, creating financial disincentives to offer telehealth services. Aligning reimbursement policies with telehealth's value and convenience is critical for its sustainable integration into healthcare systems.

Technical difficulties, such as connectivity issues, software problems, and hardware malfunctions, can significantly disrupt telehealth and telemedicine services.[7] Unstable internet connections or low bandwidth, particularly in rural or remote areas, can lead to poor video or audio quality during virtual consultations, hindering effective communication between healthcare providers and patients. Problems with the telehealth platform, such as bugs or compatibility issues with various devices, can disrupt services and cause frustration. Additionally, issues with the devices used for telehealth services can prevent patients and healthcare providers from connecting or sharing necessary medical data. To mitigate these challenges, it is essential to have robust technical support and infrastructure, including reliable internet connections, user-friendly software platforms, functional hardware, stringent data security measures, and transparent legal and regulatory guidelines. Contingency plans to address potential digital issues are also vital.

Protecting patient data is of paramount importance in telehealth and telemedicine. Any privacy or security breach can have severe consequences for patients and healthcare providers. Robust encryption, secure data storage, and strict adherence to privacy regulations are necessary to maintain patient trust and ensure the confidentiality of medical information.[6]

Not all patients may be comfortable or willing to embrace telehealth and telemedicine. Some may prefer face-to-face interactions with their healthcare providers. Additionally, disparities in access to technology and digital literacy can limit the reach of telehealth services. Addressing these challenges requires improving patient education, enhancing user-friendly telehealth platforms, and expanding access to necessary technology, particularly among vulnerable populations.

Telehealth and telemedicine offer immense potential to revolutionize healthcare delivery, and addressing these challenges is crucial for their successful implementation. Collaborative efforts from policymakers, healthcare organizations, technology providers, and communities are needed to create a regulatory framework, improve infrastructure, enhance training, align reimbursement models, ensure technical reliability, strengthen data security, and promote equitable access.[7] By overcoming these hurdles, telehealth and telemedicine can fulfill their promise of increasing healthcare access and improving patient outcomes while maintaining the highest standards of care.

Using Telehealth and Telemedicine to Improve Patient Care

Nurses are pivotal in harnessing the potential of telehealth and telemedicine to elevate patient care to new levels. Their roles in remote patient monitoring, education and support, real-time communication, and care coordination contribute significantly to improved healthcare outcomes and patient satisfaction.[1] One of the primary roles of nurses in telehealth and telemedicine is remote patient monitoring. Through the use of remote monitoring devices and telehealth platforms, nurses can keep a watchful eye on patients from a distance.[8] For individuals with chronic conditions, this means continuously tracking vital signs, symptoms, and other relevant data. When anomalies or concerning trends arise, nurses can promptly intervene or alert the patient's healthcare team, enabling real-time adjustments to treatment plans and potentially preventing exacerbation or hospitalization.

Telehealth and telemedicine also serve as invaluable tools for patient education and support. Nurses can use these technologies to provide patients with information, resources, and guidance on managing their conditions. Whether explaining medication regimens, dietary recommendations, or lifestyle changes, nurses can ensure that patients are well-informed and empowered to take an active role in their healthcare. This education and support can significantly enhance patients' ability to self-manage their conditions and make healthier choices.

In acute care, telehealth and telemedicine enable nurses to deliver timely interventions and consultations for patients facing urgent situations. In emergencies, such as strokes or cardiac events, nurses can connect with physicians and specialists in real time, facilitating rapid assessments and decisions on patient care. This agility in communication can lead to quicker, more efficient care delivery, which is often critical in emergencies where every second counts. It not only improves outcomes but also reduces the strain on healthcare resources.

Beyond individual patient care, telehealth and telemedicine have a broader impact on care coordination and collaboration among healthcare providers. Nurses can use these technologies to communicate seamlessly with other care team members, including physicians, pharmacists, physical therapists, and specialists. This level of coordination ensures that everyone involved in a patient's care is on the same page, leading to smoother transitions of care and a more holistic approach. Consequently, improved communication can help prevent errors and enhance the overall quality of care.

Moreover, the benefits of telehealth and telemedicine extend to reducing hospital readmissions and improving patient outcomes. By delivering remote monitoring and education, nurses empower patients to manage their conditions effectively, lowering the risk of complications and subsequent hospitalizations.[9] The convenience and accessibility of telehealth services also promote patient engagement and adherence to treatment plans, which can significantly boost patient satisfaction and overall wellbeing. [9]

In conclusion, nurses are at the forefront of leveraging telehealth and telemedicine to enhance patient care. Their roles encompass remote monitoring, education, real-time communication, and care coordination, all of which contribute to better healthcare outcomes, reduced hospitalizations, and higher patient satisfaction. As these technologies continue to advance, nurses will remain integral in utilizing them to their full potential, ensuring that patients receive the best possible care, regardless of location or condition.

Virtual Nursing Practice

Virtual nursing is an innovative approach to healthcare delivery that leverages technology and incorporates nurses into hospital-based patient care through telehealth.[10] Virtual nursing is a progressive healthcare model that leverages technology to extend the reach and efficiency of advanced practice nurses. These professionals are integrated into the patient care process via telehealth, ensuring that quality healthcare is accessible even from a distance. The virtual nurse operates from a command center, separate from the patient care unit, but remains integral to the healthcare delivery team. The core roles of a virtual nurse include admission and discharge, patient education and safety surveillance, staff mentoring, and physician rounding.[10] Virtual nurses play a pivotal role in various aspects of healthcare delivery. They educate patients about their health conditions, treatment options, and self-care strategies, offering immediate information and assistance through telecommunication technologies. They also mentor hospital staff by offering guidance, sharing expertise, and promoting best practices in patient care through virtual consultations. In addition, virtual nurses monitor patients' safety remotely, ensuring adherence to safety protocols and immediate response to any emerging issues. They participate in interdisciplinary rounding, contributing insights and observations that enhance patient assessment and care planning. Virtual nurses are also involved in the admission process, ensuring seamless integration of patients into the care system while capturing essential data for personalized care. Finally, they oversee the discharge process, ensuring patients are well-informed and prepared for post-hospitalization care (Figure 6.1).

Incorporating virtual nursing into patient care ensures that expertise is always accessible, enhancing patient outcomes while optimizing resource utilization. This approach to healthcare is particularly beneficial in areas with limited access to advanced healthcare facilities or professionals.

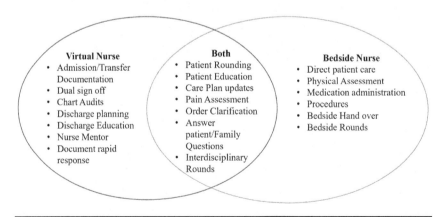

Figure 6.1 Virtual nurse model: suggested division of care team responsibilities.

It also allows for continuous monitoring and immediate response, which is critical in managing chronic conditions or acute health crises.

Impact on Patient Care

Virtual nursing models can improve patient care by constantly connecting patients and healthcare providers. This model allows for better patient safety surveillance, more effective patient education, and smoother admissions and discharges. It also enables active partnerships with patients and families in care, associated with greater patient satisfaction.

Virtual nursing models provide a constant connection between patients and healthcare providers. This is possible using telehealth technologies that allow for real-time communication and monitoring. This constant connection can lead to quicker response times to patient needs, more timely treatment plan adjustments, and improved patient outcomes.

With virtual nursing, patient safety surveillance is enhanced. Nurses can remotely monitor patients' vital signs, medication adherence, and overall health status. This allows for early detection of potential health issues and immediate intervention, improving patient safety.

Virtual nursing models can provide more effective patient education. Nurses can use digital tools to deliver educational materials, conduct virtual teaching sessions, and answer patient questions in real time. This can lead to better patient understanding of their health conditions and treatments and improved self-care behaviors.

Virtual nursing can streamline the admissions and discharge process. Nurses can coordinate care, prepare the necessary documentation, and provide discharge instructions remotely, making the process smoother and less stressful for patients. Virtual nursing models promote active partnerships with patients and families in care, leading to greater patient engagement, improved satisfaction, and better health outcomes. It also allows family members to be more involved in the patient's care, which can provide additional support and improve safety.

Addressing Workforce Challenges

Virtual nursing models are a unique approach to staffing shortages that can improve patient care.[11] Experts believe one answer to the staffing shortage may be implementing virtual nursing programs within hospitals. The COVID-19 pandemic, the retirement of baby boomer nurses, a rising aging population, and a lack of nurse educators have led to a critical shortage of nursing staff.[12] Virtual nursing models can help mitigate this shortage by allowing nurses to care for more patients remotely.

Implementing virtual nursing programs within hospitals should involve seamless integration with existing systems, comprehensive training programs for nurses, investment in robust technology infrastructure, ensuring compliance with policy and regulation, and educating patients on engaging with virtual nursing platforms. [11]

Future of Virtual Nursing

The virtual nursing model is still in its infancy, and there has yet to be a universal approach. Virtual nursing programs offer a unique blend of clinical practice and technology use. Therefore, nursing education must incorporate training in relevant technologies and telecommunication tools. This includes teaching students how to use various software platforms, understanding the nuances of virtual communication, and troubleshooting common technical issues. Moreover, virtual nursing involves significant remote patient monitoring and data analysis. Therefore, nursing schools should focus on enhancing students' skills. This could involve courses or modules on data interpretation, patient safety surveillance, and digital tools for patient assessment. The role of virtual nurses extends beyond patient care to include staff mentoring and participation in administrative tasks like admissions and discharge. Preparing students for these responsibilities will require a broad curriculum that covers leadership, team collaboration, and administrative procedures. The rise of virtual nursing programs presents a unique opportunity for nursing schools to innovate their curricula and train a new generation of nurses who are well-equipped to meet the demands of modern healthcare.

Virtual nursing models leverage advanced technology, particularly telehealth, to extend the reach and impact of nursing care. This allows nurses to provide care remotely in collaboration with the in-person care team. Virtual nursing models can improve patient safety by providing a constant connection between patients and healthcare providers. They allow for real-time monitoring of patients, early detection of potential health issues, and immediate intervention. This can result in better health outcomes. Virtual nursing models can also lead to greater patient and family satisfaction. By enabling active partnerships with patients and families in care, these models can lead to a better understanding of the treatment plan, improved adherence to medication and care routines, and ultimately, better health outcomes.

The healthcare sector, particularly nursing, is facing significant workforce challenges. These include staffing shortages due to the retirement of baby boomer nurses, the increased demand due to a rising aging population, and the impact of global health crises like the COVID-19 pandemic.[12] Virtual nursing models can help address these challenges by allowing for more efficient use of nursing resources.

Virtual nursing models can potentially transform the future of nursing by addressing current challenges and improving patient care. They represent a new way of delivering healthcare more in tune with the digital age. However, successfully implementing these models requires several key elements: adequate nurse training, a robust telehealth infrastructure, and supportive policies. While virtual nursing models present a promising solution to many challenges facing healthcare today, their successful implementation will require careful planning, significant investment in training, robust telehealth infrastructure, and supportive healthcare policies.

Conclusion

The fields of telehealth and telemedicine are experiencing rapid growth, ushering in a transformative era in healthcare delivery. Telehealth broadly encompasses using digital technology to deliver healthcare services from a distance. At the same time, telemedicine focuses on employing digital technology for diagnosing, treating, and managing medical conditions.

One of the most prominent advantages of telehealth and telemedicine is their ability to enhance healthcare access. Individuals residing in rural or remote areas and those facing mobility challenges benefit from these technologies as they grant access to specialized medical services and expertise that would otherwise be geographically out of reach. Furthermore, telehealth and telemedicine can potentially curtail healthcare expenses by eliminating the necessity for patients to embark on physical journeys to appointments and reducing hospital admissions.

Another compelling attribute of telehealth and telemedicine is their capacity to foster heightened patient engagement. These technologies empower patients by enabling them to actively monitor their health and engage in real-time communication with healthcare providers. Such enablement inspires patients to take on an active role in managing their health and wellbeing.

Nevertheless, despite their many advantages, telehealth and telemedicine introduce specific challenges. One of the most significant hurdles is the absence of standardized regulations and guidelines. Given the dynamic nature of these technologies, there is an imperative need for comprehensive and consistent regulatory frameworks that safeguard patient safety and privacy.

Additionally, healthcare providers must navigate the demands of adapting to novel technologies and workflows. Successfully incorporating telehealth and telemedicine into existing practices necessitates comprehensive training and education initiatives. These endeavors aim to ensure that healthcare providers are comfortable and proficient in employing these technologies effectively and seamlessly integrating them into their daily routines.

In summary, the burgeoning domains of telehealth and telemedicine are reshaping healthcare delivery with numerous benefits and, simultaneously, specific challenges. Nurses are pivotal in leveraging these technologies to enhance patient care in this transformative landscape. They contribute by remotely monitoring patients, offering education and support, and engaging in real-time communication with patients and fellow healthcare providers. Through their proactive involvement, nurses can harness the potential of telehealth and telemedicine to optimize patient outcomes and healthcare accessibility.

References

1. Rutledge C, Gustin T. Preparing nurses for roles in telehealth: now is the time! Online J Issue Nurs. 2021;26(1). https://doi.org/10.3912/OJIN.Vol26No01Man03.
2. Koonin LM, Hoots B, Tsang CA, Leroy, Z, Farris, K, Jolly, BT, Antall, P, McCabe, B, Zelis, C, Tong, I, Harris, AMl. Trends in the use of telehealth during the emergence of the COVID-19 pandemic—United States. MMWR Morb Mortal Wkly Rep. 2020;69:1595–1599. DOI: http://dx.doi.org/10.15585/mmwr.mm6943a3.
3. Hasselfeld BW. *Benefits of telemedicine*, n.d. www.hopkinsm edicine.org/health/treatment-tests-and-therapies/Benefits-of-Telemedicine.
4. Watson S. *Telehealth the advantages and disadvantages*, 2020. www.health.harvard.edu/staying-healthy/telehealth-the-advanta ges-and-disadvantages.
5. Aime M. *Telehealth vs. telemedicine: what's the difference?*, 2023. www.goodrx.com/healthcare-access/telehealth/telehea lth-vs-telemedicine.
6. Bradley J. *Telehealth today: challenges & opportunities*, 2020. Retrieved from https://aihc-assn.org/telehealth-today-challen ges-opportunities/.
7. Ftouni R, AlJardali B, Hamdanieh M, Ftouni L, Salem N. Challenges of telemedicine during the COVID-19 pandemic: a systematic review. BMC Med Informat Decision Mak. 2022;22(1):1–21. https://doi.org/10.1186/s12 911-022-01952-0.

8. The Rising Role of Telemedicine and What It Means to Nurses, 2021. Retrieved from https://nursingonline.pnw.edu/programs/telemedicine-nursing/.

9. Deering M. What are the pros and cons of telehealth nursing? Nurse J. 2022. https://nursejournal.org/careers/telehealth-nurse/pros-and-cons/.

10. Sanford K, Schuelke S, Lee M, Mossburg S. *Virtual nursing: improving patient care and meeting workforce challenges*, 2023. Retrieved from https://psnet.ahrq.gov/pers pective/virtual-nursing-improving-patient-care-and-meeting-workforce-challenges.

11. Morris G. *Hospitals launch virtual nursing programs to address workforce issues*, 2023. Retrieved from https://nursejournal.org/articles/what-is-virtual-nursing/.

12. Wintemute D. *Virtual nursing: can a first-of-its-kind hospital program help address nursing shortage and burnout?*, 2023. Retrieved from https://nursejournal.org/articles/virtual-nursing/.

Chapter 7

Mobile Health (mHealth)

History and Evolution of mHealth

Mobile health, also called mHealth, has traversed a remarkable journey since its inception. In the early 2000s, the primary focus of mHealth revolved around employing short message service (SMS)–based interventions to disseminate health information and reminders to patients, particularly in regions with limited healthcare resources. This approach successfully enhanced maternal and child health outcomes across several countries. The maiden pilot project utilizing SMS was initiated in South Africa, targeting pregnant women to provide them with pertinent health information. These SMS messages were thoughtfully designed to offer support and informative content tailored to the specific stage of pregnancy and the child's age as part of the Mobile Alliance for Maternal Action (MAMA) South Africa project.[1]

DOI: 10.4324/9781003439721-7

Over time, mHealth has evolved significantly, transitioning from SMS-based interventions to more advanced mobile applications and wearable devices. As mobile technology progressed, so did the capabilities of mHealth. The advent of smartphones and mobile applications empowered healthcare providers to offer more sophisticated interventions, including telemedicine consultations, remote patient monitoring, and medication adherence reminders.[2]

With the proliferation of smartphones and the availability of high-speed internet, mHealth has become increasingly accessible to the general public. Presently, a vast array of health-related mobile applications are available, spanning from fitness tracking to comprehensive disease management. The utilization of wearable devices, such as fitness trackers and smartwatches, has experienced a surge in popularity in recent years. These devices can monitor a broad spectrum of health metrics, encompassing physical activity, heart rate, and sleep patterns. They provide patients valuable insights into their wellbeing and enable healthcare providers to monitor patients remotely.

Beyond patient-centric applications, mHealth has also played a pivotal role in enhancing healthcare delivery and efficiency. Mobile applications have been developed to assist healthcare providers in tasks like medication management, appointment scheduling, and electronic health record (EHR) documentation. These applications offer the advantage of precise and timely documentation, ensuring healthcare providers and patients have a secure platform for sharing patient data to inform decision-making regarding care and treatment plans.

The emergence of the COVID-19 pandemic further accelerated the integration of mHealth, as both patients and healthcare providers were encouraged to embrace remote communication and care delivery to mitigate the risk of infection. With the ongoing expansion and evolution of mobile technology, the potential of mHealth to revolutionize healthcare delivery and enhance patient outcomes is boundless.

Benefits of Using mHealth

mHealth offers many advantages, including improved access to healthcare, potential cost savings, and heightened patient engagement. It empowers patients to harness the capabilities of mobile devices to monitor their symptoms, access health-related information, and tap into valuable resources, all at their convenience and regardless of their location, thus diminishing the necessity for in-person consultations. Benefits of mHealth include improved access to healthcare, cost savings, and increased patient engagement.[3] While mHealth holds the promise of reducing healthcare costs, further research and conclusive evidence are required to solidify this potential.

One of the paramount merits of mHealth lies in its ability to augment access to healthcare services, particularly benefiting individuals residing in remote or rural areas.[4] By harnessing mobile devices, healthcare providers can extend their services to patients who face barriers to physical travel, bridging geographical barriers and ensuring equitable access to care. Patients in remote or rural areas can receive medical advice, schedule appointments, or even consult with healthcare professionals through mobile applications. This is particularly beneficial for individuals who may not have easy access to healthcare facilities.

Enhancing patient engagement is another cornerstone of mHealth. Patients are empowered with greater control over their health and treatment regimens through mobile applications that enable them to track their health status, receive timely medication reminders, and communicate in real time with healthcare professionals. This heightened engagement translates into potentially improved health outcomes as patients become active partners in their care.

Furthermore, mHealth catalyzes fortified communication between patients and healthcare providers. Patients can effortlessly reach out to their healthcare teams through mobile devices, facilitating inquiries, symptom reporting, and the swift exchange of guidance. This open communication channel fosters higher levels of patient satisfaction, as individuals feel more deeply involved in their care and are equipped with a comprehensive understanding of their conditions and treatments. Moreover, it can improve coordination among healthcare providers, ensuring a more holistic approach to patient care.

In resource-limited settings, mHealth takes on the role of a transformative tool that enhances healthcare delivery. Mobile applications equip healthcare providers with access to medical references, patient data, and training materials, elevating the quality of care they offer. Additionally, mobile devices facilitate the seamless collection and transmission of patient data, simplifying the monitoring and tracking of healthcare outcomes.

Lastly, mHealth contributes to the promotion of public health by serving as a vehicle for health awareness and disease prevention.[5] Health-focused mobile applications inform users with knowledge about healthy behaviors, encompassing elements like diet and exercise, and actively encourage individuals to embrace positive lifestyle changes. Moreover, mHealth can play a pivotal role in controlling and tracking infectious diseases by furnishing real-time data on disease outbreaks, contact tracing, disseminating accurate information, and monitoring disease spread. In sum, mHealth embodies a multifaceted approach to healthcare that holds immense potential to revolutionize healthcare delivery and management. Harnessing the power of mobile technology can make healthcare more accessible, efficient, and patient-centered while promoting broader public health initiatives (Table 7.1).

Table 7.1   mHealth Benefits

mHealth Benefit	Explanation
Improved access to care	Mobile health (mHealth) technologies enable patients to quickly send secure messages, schedule appointments, and connect to healthcare providers 24/7 for telemedicine visits. mHealth clinics can bring needed health services directly to underserved populations.
Cost savings	mHealth clinics provide quality care at a lower cost than traditional healthcare delivery modes. They help patients avoid expensive emergency room visits and provide cost-effective prevention services.
Improved medication adherence	mHealth apps and technology solutions improve medication adherence by giving patients features such as automated medication and refill reminders, and educational information.
Remote patient monitoring	Remote patient monitoring enables patients to use mobile devices and mHealth technology to gather, enter, or automatically collect health data and transmit it to healthcare providers.
Preventive services	Mobile clinics can provide more preventive services such as cholesterol tests, blood pressure checks, and early detection of diseases.
Improved communication	mHealth improves communication between patients and healthcare providers, leading to fewer hospital visits, reduced patient costs, and improved access.

Challenges of Using mHealth

While teeming with potential, the mHealth domain is fraught with numerous challenges that must be addressed to harness its transformative power in healthcare fully. These challenges span a broad spectrum, including regulatory, technological, human factors, privacy, information management, and access-related issues.[6]

One of the main challenges is the lack of regulation and standardization for mHealth applications, leading to inconsistencies in the quality of care provided. As the field is still in its early stages, there is a need for guidelines and regulations to ensure that mHealth applications and tools are safe and effective. In addition, standardization is needed to ensure that different mHealth applications and tools can work together seamlessly. Establishing robust regulatory frameworks and industry standards is crucial to ensure the safety and efficacy of mHealth applications and foster seamless interoperability among different tools.[6]

Another significant concern is the necessity for reliable internet access. Using mHealth requires a reliable and secure internet connection, which may not be available in all areas. While mHealth thrives on the backbone of secure, high-speed internet, many regions, especially remote or underserved areas, struggle with inconsistent access. Bridging this digital divide is indispensable to extend equitable healthcare delivery through mHealth solutions.[7]

Healthcare providers face a significant challenge in incorporating mHealth into their workflows. They must be skilled in using mobile devices, communicating through these platforms, and providing remote care. Therefore, extensive training and continuous support for healthcare professionals to use mHealth tools effectively are crucial.

Design and user needs assessment also dominate the mHealth landscape. Some applications are designed without sufficient regard for scientific foundations and may fail to address user needs. A rigorous assessment of user needs and adherence to evidence-based design principles are fundamental in crafting effective and user-friendly mHealth solutions.

The paramount issue of privacy and data security demands unwavering attention. Collecting and sharing sensitive patient information on mobile devices and applications introduce significant privacy and security concerns. The ever-present threat of cyberattacks and data breaches necessitates the implementation of robust policies, encryption, and stringent security measures to safeguard patient data within the mHealth ecosystem.

With so many health-related mobile applications and resources available, a possible risk emerges—too much information. Patients may face an overload of health information, which could cause uncertainty and detachment from healthcare providers. The answer is to simplify information delivery and encourage verified, reliable sources to address this issue.[8]

Lastly, the promise of mHealth's potential to improve healthcare access is tinged with the risk of exacerbating healthcare disparities. Low-income and underserved communities may lack access to smartphones and dependable internet connections, hindering their ability to harness the benefits of mHealth technologies. Initiatives aimed at ensuring equitable access, such as subsidized smartphone programs or community Wi-Fi initiatives, are indispensable in thwarting disparities in healthcare outcomes.[8]

Addressing these multifaceted challenges necessitates concerted efforts, calling for collaboration between healthcare stakeholders, technology developers, policymakers, and regulatory bodies. By navigating these obstacles with determination and innovation, mHealth can continue evolving as a potent force, poised to enhance healthcare delivery, elevate patient outcomes, and render healthcare more accessible to all.[6]

Using mHealth to Improve Patient Care

Nurses are essential contributors to using the potential of mHealth to improve patient care, and their role covers a broad range of vital functions within healthcare delivery. By integrating mobile applications and wearable devices, nurses can revolutionize how patient care is administered and experienced.[9] First and foremost, nurses can harness mHealth solutions to monitor patient health with unprecedented precision. Mobile applications offer a platform through which vital signs, symptoms, and health data can be continuously tracked, empowering nurses to detect subtle changes in a patient's condition in real time. This early recognition of deviations enables swift responses and interventions, potentially averting complications and improving patient outcomes.

Moreover, mHealth has become an indispensable tool in the nurse's arsenal when managing chronic conditions. Mobile applications and wearable devices provide an avenue for meticulously tracking vital signs and symptom patterns. With this data at their fingertips, nurses can proactively manage chronic conditions, providing timely support and education to patients as needed. This enhances patient wellbeing and encourages patients to become active participants in their own care, leading to more effective self-management of their conditions.

Beyond chronic condition management, mHealth empowers nurses to elevate patient care in myriad ways.

Mobile applications can deliver patients personalized health information, reminders, and alerts, ensuring they stay engaged and informed throughout their healthcare journey. Nurses can also utilize these applications to streamline communication with fellow healthcare providers, facilitating appointment scheduling, sharing vital medical records, and fostering seamless collaboration on patient care plans. This cohesive approach to healthcare delivery enhances overall care quality and coordination.

Furthermore, mHealth bolsters patient engagement by offering patients direct access to health information and resources via mobile devices. Patients can use these tools to educate themselves about their conditions, track symptoms, manage medications, and receive personalized nutrition advice. This level of engagement empowers patients to make informed decisions about their health, leading to improved health outcomes.[9]

Real-time communication facilitated by mHealth is another facet that benefits nurses and patients. Patients can readily contact their healthcare providers whenever concerns arise, leading to timely interventions and enhanced care coordination. This proactive communication fosters a partnership between patients and healthcare providers, resulting in a more patient-centered approach to care.[10]

Finally, mHealth contributes to the efficiency and effectiveness of healthcare delivery by automating routine tasks that were once time-consuming. Mobile applications can manage tasks like appointment scheduling and medication refills, freeing up nurses' valuable time to focus on providing personalized and patient-centric care. This streamlined workflow reduces administrative burdens and ensures that nurses can allocate their expertise where it matters most— directly supporting patients in their healthcare journeys.

Nurses equipped with mHealth tools can revolutionize patient care by delivering proactive, personalized, and efficient healthcare services. This transformation improves patient outcomes and enriches the overall healthcare experience for both patients and healthcare providers.

Nurse informaticists are pivotal in adopting and integrating mHealth into healthcare systems. Their role is multifaceted, encompassing a range of responsibilities that bridge the gap between healthcare and technology. Nurse informaticists leverage their clinical experience and technical knowledge to ensure that mHealth solutions are effectively integrated into healthcare practices. They understand healthcare providers' unique needs and workflows, allowing them to adapt mHealth solutions to these specific needs. This ensures that the technology enhances, rather than disrupts, existing healthcare practices. Nurse informaticists are involved in designing, implementing, and evaluating mHealth applications. They work closely with software developers and information technology professionals to create user-friendly, safe applications that satisfy the needs of patients and healthcare providers. They also play a crucial role in testing these applications and gathering user feedback to make necessary improvements.

Nurse informaticists provide training and support to other healthcare professionals using these technologies. This is essential in promoting the adoption and utilization of mHealth solutions. Practical training and continuous support help alleviate any fears or reservations healthcare providers may have about using new technologies.

Nurse informaticists facilitate communication and data sharing through mHealth solutions. This can lead to improved patient outcomes, as healthcare providers have access to real-time patient data, enabling them to make informed decisions about patient care. It can also increase efficiency, reducing the need for manual data entry and allowing for more streamlined communication between healthcare providers.

The role of nurse informaticists is vital in the digital transformation of healthcare. As healthcare systems increasingly adopt digital technologies, the need for professionals who can navigate these systems' clinical and technical aspects is paramount. Nurse informaticists are ideally positioned to fulfill this role, given their unique blend of clinical experience and technical expertise.

In conclusion, nurse informaticists play a crucial role in adopting mHealth, acting as a bridge between healthcare and technology, and contributing to improved patient outcomes, increased efficiency, and the advancement of mHealth solutions. Their role is vital in the digital transformation of healthcare, and their work is instrumental in shaping the future of healthcare delivery (Figure 7.1).

Conclusion

Mobile health, or mHealth, is an innovative field that has the potential to transform healthcare by leveraging the use of mobile devices, such as smartphones and tablets, to deliver healthcare services and information. With the widespread adoption of mobile devices, mHealth is becoming increasingly popular to improve access to healthcare services and reduce costs, especially in low- and middle-income countries where traditional healthcare infrastructure is lacking. Despite these benefits, mHealth also presents several challenges. One of the biggest challenges is the lack of regulation and standardization.

Nurses can play a crucial role in improving patient care through mHealth. Nurses can use mobile devices to monitor patient health, provide education and support, and

Figure 7.1   Conceptual diagram of mHealth. (Modified from Fleming JN, Treiber F, McGillicuddy J, Gebregziabher M, Taber DJ. Improving transplant medication safety through a pharmacist-empowered, patient-centered, mHealth-based intervention: TRANSAFE Rx study protocol. JMIR Res Protocols. 2018;7(3). https://doi.org/10.2196/resprot.9078.)

communicate with patients and other healthcare providers in real time. For example, nurses can use mHealth applications to track patient vital signs and medication adherence, provide patient education and support, and communicate with patients and other healthcare providers to ensure that care is coordinated and effective.

In conclusion, mHealth is a rapidly growing field that has the potential to transform healthcare by leveraging the use of mobile devices to deliver healthcare services and information. While mHealth presents several challenges, including the lack of regulation and standardization and the need for healthcare providers to adapt to new technologies and workflows, it also presents significant opportunities to improve patient care.

Nurses can play a crucial role in using mHealth to improve patient care by monitoring patient health, providing education and support, and communicating with patients and other healthcare providers in real time.

References

1. Lau YK, Cassidy T, Hacking D, Brittain, K, Haricharan, HJ, Heap. M. Antenatal health promotion via short message service at a Midwife Obstetrics Unit in South Africa: a mixed methods study. BMC Pregnancy Childbirth. 2014;14:284. https://doi.org/10.1186/1471-2393-14-284.

2. Beaton T. *Top 10 healthcare mobile apps among hospital, health systems,* 2017. Retrieved from https://mhealthintelligence.com/news/mhealth-interventions-streamline-provider-caregiver-man agement.

3. Rowland SP, Fitzgerald JE, Holme T, Powell, J, McGregor, A. What is the clinical value of mHealth for patients? NPJ Digit Med. 2020;3:4. https://doi.org/10.1038/s41746-019-0206-x.

4. Woodall T, Ramage M, LaBruyere JT, McLean W, Tak CR. Telemedicine services during COVID-19: considerations for medically underserved populations. J Rural Health. 2021;37(1):231–234. https://doi.org/10.1111/jrh.12466.

5. O'Connell J, Abbas M, Beecham S, Buckley J, Chochlov M, Fitzgerald B, Glynn L, Johnson K, Laffey J, McNicholas B, Nuseibeh B, O'Callaghan M, O'Keeffe I, Razzaq A, Rekanar K, Richardson I, Simpkin A, Storni C, Tsvyatkova D, Walsh J, Welsh T, O'Keeffe D. Best practice guidance for digital contact tracing apps: a cross-disciplinary review of the literature. JMIR Mhealth Uhealth 2021;9(6):e27753. doi: 10.2196/27753.

6. Collier J. *mHealth: What is it, and how can it help us?,* 2018. Retrieved from www.medicalnewstoday.com/articles/322865.

7. Solomon Nsor-Anabiah I, Udunwa MU, Malathi S, Supervisor PD, Nsor-Anabiah S. Review of the prospects and challenges of mHealth implementation in developing countries. Int J Appl Eng Res. 2019;14:2897–2903. www.ripublication.com.

8. Resources for Mobile Health Apps Developers, n.d. Retrieved September 22, 2023, from www.hhs.gov/hipaa/for-profession als/special-topics/health-apps/index.html.

9. Madanian S, Parry DT, Airehrour D, Cherrington M. mHealth and big-data integration: promises for healthcare system in India. BMJ Health Care Inform. 2019;26(1):1–8. https://doi.org/ 10.1136/bmjhci-2019-100071.

10. Fortuin J, Salie F, Abdullahi LH, Douglas TS. The impact of mHealth interventions on health systems: a systematic review protocol. Syst Rev. 2016;5(1):1–6. https://doi.org/10.1186/s13 643-016-0387-1.

Chapter 8

Ethical and Legal Issues in Nursing Informatics

Privacy and Security

Privacy and security are crucial considerations in nursing informatics because electronic health records (EHRs) and other health information technologies contain sensitive personal and medical information that must be protected from unauthorized access and disclosure. Patients have the right to control who has access to their health information, and nurses have an ethical obligation to protect patient privacy.[1]

Privacy refers to the right of individuals to control access to their personal information, including their health information. In healthcare, privacy is protected by laws and regulations such as the Health Insurance Portability and Accountability Act (HIPAA)[2] in the United States and the General Data Protection Regulation (GDPR)[3] in the European Union. These

 DOI: 10.4324/9781003439721-8

laws and regulations set standards for collecting, using, and disclosing personal information, including health information.

Security refers to protecting personal information from unauthorized access, use, disclosure, modification, or destruction. Security measures can include physical, technical, and administrative safeguards, such as access controls, encryption, and employee training. Healthcare organizations are required to implement security measures to protect patient information, especially when it is stored electronically as protected health information (PHI). One key measure is access controls, which ensure only authorized personnel can access PHI. This often involves unique user identification, emergency access procedures, automatic logoff, and encryption.

Physical safeguards are also necessary, including facility access controls, workstation use and security, and device and media controls. These measures limit physical access to facilities and workstations that can access PHI. Technical safeguards involve using technology to protect PHI and control access to it. This often includes access control, audit controls, integrity controls, and transmission security.

Network security protects against unauthorized access to the network or network-accessible information. This includes the use of firewalls and other security measures. HIPAA also requires covered entities to conduct a risk analysis and manage potential risks and vulnerabilities to the confidentiality, integrity, and availability of PHI.[2]

Training and awareness initiatives are crucial, with employees trained on the importance of protecting patient information and the specific measures the organization has put in place. Finally, healthcare organizations are required to implement reasonable and appropriate policies and procedures to comply with the standards, implementation specifications, and other requirements. These measures are not exhaustive and may vary based on the specific needs and capabilities of each healthcare organization. Nurses play a crucial role in ensuring these measures are followed in their practice.

Nurses must be familiar with the regulations and standards related to privacy and security in their organization and jurisdiction and ensure that these are followed in their practice. This includes understanding patients' rights regarding their health information, obtaining informed consent for the collection, use, and disclosure of health information, and using secure systems and procedures to protect health information. Nurses must also be aware of the potential risks and vulnerabilities associated with health information technologies and take steps to minimize these risks. This includes using strong passwords, avoiding sharing login credentials, and promptly reporting any security incidents or breaches.

Privacy and security are critical issues in nursing informatics, as electronic health records and other health information technologies contain sensitive personal and medical information that must be protected from unauthorized access and disclosure. Nurses have an ethical obligation to protect patients' privacy. By taking steps to protect patient privacy and security, nurses can help ensure patient information is kept safe and secure.

Patient privacy and security are critical issues in nursing informatics. Nurses must ensure that patient data is collected, stored, and transmitted securely to protect patient privacy and prevent data breaches. This involves following established security protocols, such as encrypting data, using secure communication channels, and implementing access controls to limit who can access patient data (Table 8.1).

Table 8.1   Measures to Protect Personal Health Information (PHI)

Measure	Description
Access controls	Designed to ensure that only authorized personnel have access to PHI. This often involves the use of unique user identification, emergency access procedures, automatic logoff, and encryption and decryption.
Physical safeguards	Include facility access controls, workstation use, workstation security, and device and media controls. They are designed to limit physical access to facilities and workstations that can access PHI.
Technical safeguards	Involve the use of technology to protect PHI and control access to it. This often includes access control, audit controls, integrity controls, and transmission security.
Network security	Used to protect against unauthorized access to the network or network-accessible information. This includes the use of firewalls and other security measures to ensure that PHI is not accessed without authorization.
Risk analysis and management	HIPAA requires covered entities to conduct an accurate and thorough assessment of the potential risks and vulnerabilities to the confidentiality, integrity, and availability of PHI.
Training and awareness	Employees are trained on the importance of protecting patient information and the specific measures the organization has implemented.
Policies and procedures	Healthcare organizations are required to implement reasonable and appropriate policies and procedures to comply with the standards, implementation specifications, and other requirements of the security rule.

Source: Health Insurance Portability and Accountability Act of 1996 (HIPAA), June 27, 2022. Retrieved from www.cdc.gov/phlp/php/resources/health-insurance-port ability-and-accountability-act-of-1996-hipaa.html?CDC_AAref_Val=https://www. cdc.gov/Phlp/Publications/Topic/Hipaa.Html.

Patient Autonomy

Patient autonomy is a fundamental principle of medical ethics that emphasizes the importance of respecting patients' rights to make decisions about their healthcare.[4] It recognizes that patients are individuals with unique values, beliefs, and preferences and should be able to make decisions about their health based on these factors. This includes the right to refuse treatment, make choices about end-of-life care, and participate in clinical research. With the increasing use of health information technologies, patients have greater access to their health information and can use it to make informed decisions about their healthcare. However, this raises ethical issues about how much information patients should access and how much control they should have over their health information.

Nurses must be familiar with the regulations and standards of nursing informatics and ensure theses are followed in their practice. This includes following ethical guidelines, such as the American Nurses Association Code of Ethics for Nurses with Interpretive Statements,[4] and complying with legal requirements, such as HIPAA regulations.[2]

Patient autonomy means that healthcare providers, including nurses, must inform patients about their medical conditions, treatment options, risks and benefits, and potential outcomes. Nurses should also help patients understand their health information, answer their questions, and support them in making informed decisions. Patients have the right to control their health information and decide who can access it. Nurses must ensure that patient data is used ethically and with the patient's consent. This includes obtaining informed consent from patients before collecting or using their data and ensuring patients have access to their health information.

Nurses must balance the patient's right to autonomy with their duty to provide accurate and complete information to patients. Patients should have access to their health information and be able to make informed decisions about their healthcare. However, nurses must ensure patients have accurate and complete information and refrain from making decisions that may harm their health.

However, patient autonomy has limits, particularly regarding decision-making capacity. Patients who lack the ability to make decisions, either temporarily or permanently, may require surrogate decision-makers, such as family members or legal guardians. Nurses must also consider the potential for patients to make decisions that may harm themselves or others, such as refusing life-saving treatment.

In addition, patient autonomy can be challenging to balance with other ethical principles, such as beneficence (doing good) and non-maleficence (avoiding harm). For example, patients may make decisions that conflict with medical advice or best practices. In these situations, nurses may need to engage in ethical deliberation and consult with colleagues and other healthcare professionals to determine the best course of action. Healthcare organizations commonly have ethics boards, which are staffed with experts and can assist with these deliberations and ensure ethical standards are followed.

Patient autonomy is a critical aspect of patient-centered care that recognizes patients' right to participate in their healthcare decisions.[5] Nurses promote patient autonomy by providing accurate and complete information, supporting patient decision-making, and advocating for patients' rights (Table 8.2).

Table 8.2 Data Harms

Data Harms	Definition
Discrimination and stigma	Data can be employed to depict individuals or groups in a manner that leads to their detriment and disadvantages.
Disempowerment	A lack of authority and influence over the secondary applications of data can result in a state of powerlessness.
Disenfranchisement	An absence of clarity and involvement concerning the secondary utilization of data can result in disenfranchisement. Users often do not know how their data is being used, which can lead to feelings of unease about how data is collected, used, and analyzed.
Exploitation	Patients or those who generate data might not reap adequate benefits from the secondary applications of clinical information. For example, users whose data is sold to third parties.
Privacy breaches	Unjustified or unauthorized intrusions into a person's personal sphere can lead to significant harm. For historically marginalized groups, the right to privacy is a matter of survival.

Source: Ballantyne A. How should we think about clinical data ownership? J Med Ethics, 2020;46(5):289–294. https://doi.org/10.1136/medethics-2018-105340.

Data Ownership

Data ownership is essential in healthcare, particularly with the increasing use of health information technologies. It refers to who owns the health information collected by these technologies and who has the right to access, use, and control it. Nurses must know who owns the data and how it can be used. Patients have the right to control their health information and decide who can access it.[6] Nurses must ensure that patient data is used ethically and with the patient's consent. This includes the right to access their health information, as well as the right to authorize or restrict others from accessing it.

However, healthcare organizations may also claim ownership of patient data, particularly if collected through their facilities or systems. In some cases, healthcare organizations may use patient data for research or other purposes, and patients may not have complete control over how their data is used. Nurses must be aware of these issues and ensure that patient data is used ethically and with the patient's consent.

Nurses have a professional responsibility to protect patient privacy and confidentiality while also providing quality care. This can involve sharing patient information with other healthcare providers to ensure patients receive appropriate care. However, nurses must ensure that patient data is only shared with those who have a legitimate need to know and that patients have given their informed consent for their data to be shared.

Additionally, nurses must ensure that patient data is collected, stored, and transmitted securely to protect patient privacy and prevent data breaches. This involves following established security protocols, such as encrypting data, using secure communication channels, and implementing access controls to limit who can access patient data.

Overall, nurses play an essential role in protecting patient data ownership and ensuring that patient data is used ethically and with the patient's consent. By following established privacy and security protocols and respecting patient autonomy, nurses can help ensure patients' rights to control their health information are respected while also providing quality care.

In the rapidly evolving healthcare landscape, the nurse informaticist is responsible for maintaining data privacy and security as they implement robust security measures to safeguard patient data. This involves working with the healthcare information technology team to ensure the use of advanced techniques such as encryption, establishing secure networks, and deploying robust authentication protocols.

In addition to the technical aspects, nurse informaticists also have a significant role in human factors related to data security. They are responsible for educating healthcare providers on the significance of data privacy and the proper methods for managing confidential patient information. This education may cover various topics, from identifying phishing attempts to knowing the value of password security and the dangers of unsecured networks.

Compliance with regulations is also critical to their role. Nurse informaticists work diligently to ensure healthcare organizations adhere to data privacy laws and regulations. In the United States, for instance, they ensure compliance with HIPAA.

Nurse informaticists' responsibilities also extend to auditing and monitoring. They may conduct regular audits and continuously monitor systems to detect any potential threats to data security and data misuse. Auditing and monitoring are critical components of a nurse informaticist's role in maintaining data privacy and security. These activities are essential for identifying potential threats to data security and instances of data misuse and ensuring compliance with data privacy regulations.

Auditing involves a systematic review of systems, procedures, and operations. Nurse informaticists may conduct regular audits to assess the effectiveness of existing security measures and policies. These audits can reveal vulnerabilities in the system, such as weak access controls or outdated software that could potentially be exploited to gain unauthorized access to patient data. Audits also help ensure that data-handling practices within the organization comply with established policies and legal requirements.

Monitoring, on the other hand, is a continuous process. Nurse informaticists may monitor healthcare information systems in real time to detect unusual or suspicious activity. This could include multiple failed login attempts, unauthorized attempts to access sensitive data, or changes to system configurations. Advanced monitoring tools can even detect patterns of behavior that may indicate a coordinated attack on the system. In addition to detecting potential threats, monitoring also helps identify instances of data misuse. This could involve healthcare staff accessing patient records without a valid reason or sharing patient information inappropriately. By detecting such instances, nurse informaticists can take immediate action to prevent further misuse and help identify the responsible parties.

Through auditing and monitoring, nurse informaticists play a vital role in maintaining the integrity of healthcare information systems. These activities allow them to proactively address potential threats to data security, ensure compliance with data privacy regulations, and protect patient data from misuse. As healthcare continues to become more digitized, the importance of these responsibilities cannot be overstated.

Policy development is another area where nurse informaticists make significant contributions. They develop, implement, and update policies and procedures related to data privacy and security, ensuring they remain relevant as technology and regulations evolve.

The process begins with the development of policies. Nurse informaticists, leveraging their unique blend of nursing and informatics knowledge, draft policies aligning with healthcare best practices and data security principles. These policies cover many areas, from access controls and data-sharing protocols to incident response plans and data backup procedures.

Once these policies are developed, the next step is implementation. This involves disseminating the policies throughout the organization, training staff on their responsibilities under these policies, and integrating the policies into daily workflows. Nurse informaticists often work closely with other departments, such as information technology and human resources, to ensure a smooth and effective implementation process.

Given the rapidly evolving nature of technology and regulatory environments, policies must be regularly reviewed and updated. Changes in technology can introduce new vulnerabilities that need to be addressed, while changes in regulations may require adjustments to ensure continued compliance. Nurse informaticists play a vital role in the ongoing process. They must stay abreast of developments in healthcare and information security and use this knowledge to make necessary updates to the organization's data privacy and security policies. This might involve adjusting procedures in response to a new threat or revising policies to incorporate new regulatory requirements.

Policy development is a dynamic and ongoing process vital to maintaining data privacy and security in healthcare settings. Through their contributions in this area, nurse informaticists help ensure that healthcare organizations can provide high-quality care while protecting the sensitive information entrusted to them. Their role in policy development is significant and indispensable.

Finally, nurse informaticists collaborate closely with information technology teams to implement technical safeguards and keep the systems up to date with the latest security software. The collaboration between nurse informaticists and information technology teams is a crucial aspect of maintaining data privacy and security in healthcare settings. This partnership leverages the unique skills and knowledge of both professions to create a comprehensive and practical approach to data security.

Nurse informaticists bring their expertise in nursing and healthcare, along with a deep understanding of the healthcare sector's specific data privacy needs and regulatory requirements. They understand the types of data that are collected in healthcare settings, the sensitivity of this data, and the potential impacts of a data breach on patients and healthcare providers.

Information technology professionals contribute their technical expertise, including knowledge of the latest security software and technologies. They understand the technical aspects of data security, from network infrastructure to software applications, and can implement technical safeguards to protect data. Together, nurse informaticists and information technology teams work to implement these technical safeguards, which may include firewalls, encryption technologies, secure servers, and intrusion-detection systems. They also ensure that the systems are kept up to date with the latest security software to protect against new and emerging threats. This collaboration extends beyond the implementation of security measures. Nurse informaticists and information technology teams also work together to monitor systems for potential security threats, respond to security-breach incidents, and recover data in the event of a breach. The collaboration between nursing informaticists and information technology teams is essential for a holistic approach to data security in healthcare settings. By combining the strengths of healthcare and information technology professionals, healthcare organizations can more effectively protect the privacy and security of patient data.

Nurse informaticists are vital to protecting the privacy and security of patient data in healthcare settings. As healthcare becomes increasingly digitized and the volume of patient data continues to grow, their role is set to become even more vital.

Conclusion

In conclusion, nursing informatics is a rapidly evolving field that involves using technology to manage and analyze health information. Nursing informatics stands at the intersection of technological advancement and patient-centered care, and it carries profound ethical and legal considerations that nurses must navigate with care and precision. Central to this evolving landscape are the fundamental principles of privacy and security, patient autonomy, and data ownership. These pillars serve as the guiding principles in the realm of nursing informatics, ensuring that the integration of health information technologies is both ethical and patient-centric.

Protecting patient privacy and safeguarding their health data are ethical imperatives. As healthcare professionals, nurses are responsible for ensuring the confidentiality and security of sensitive medical information. By adhering to stringent privacy regulations and implementing robust security measures, nurses can cultivate an environment where patients can trust that their health data is handled with the utmost care and respect.

Patient autonomy, a cornerstone of modern healthcare, extends seamlessly into the digital realm. Nurses must remain vigilant in empowering patients to make informed decisions regarding collecting, using, and disclosing their health information. Respecting patients' autonomy entails obtaining informed consent, providing transparency in data practices, and advocating patients' rights to control their health data.

Furthermore, the question of data ownership becomes pivotal in nursing informatics. Nurses must be cognizant of the legal frameworks and standards governing the acquisition and utilization of health data. This awareness ensures that data ownership remains unambiguous, protecting patients' rights while fostering responsible data stewardship.

Nursing informatics is a dynamic field that promises to revolutionize healthcare delivery. However, the ethical and legal considerations accompanying these technological advancements require nurses and nurse informaticists to become informed and vigilant patient advocates. By adhering to best practices, staying current with regulations and standards, and consistently advocating for patient rights, nurses can help shape a future where health information technologies enhance patient care, safeguard privacy, and uphold patient autonomy. In doing so, they fulfill their professional obligations and moral duty to serve as the guardians of ethical and responsible nursing informatics.

References

1. McBride S, Tietze M, Robichaux C, Stokes L, Weber E. Identifying and addressing ethical issues with use of electronic health records. Online J Issues Nursing. 2018;23(1):Manuscript 5.
2. Health Insurance Portability and Accountability Act of 1996 (HIPAA), June 27, 2022. www.cdc.gov/phlp/php/resources/health-insurance-portability-and-accountability-act-of-1996-hipaa.html?CDC_AAref_Val=https://www.cdc.gov/Phlp/Publications/Topic/Hipaa.Html.
3. What Is GDPR, the EU's New Data Protection Law?, n.d. Retrieved on October 14, 2023, from https://gdpr.eu/what-is-gdpr/.

4. Code of Ethics for Nurses: With Interpretive Statements. American Nurses Association, 2015. Retrieved from www.nursi ngworld.org/practice-policy/nursing-excellence/ethics/code-of-ethics-for-nurses/.

5. Raus K, Mortier E, Eeckloo K. The patient perspective in health care networks. BMC Med Ethics. 2018;19:52. https://doi.org/10.1186/s12910-018-0298-x.

6. Ballantyne A. How should we think about clinical data ownership? J Med Ethics. 2020;46(5):289–294. https://doi.org/10.1136/medethics-2018-105340.

Chapter 9

Training and Education in Nursing Informatics

Certifications in Nursing Informatics

Certifications in nursing informatics demonstrate that nurses have acquired specialized knowledge and skills in the field of nursing informatics. The Nursing Informatics-Board Certified (NI-BC) certification is a prestigious credential offered by the American Nurses Credentialing Center (ANCC). This certification is designed to validate the entry-level clinical knowledge and skills of registered nurses in the nursing informatics specialty after obtaining their initial registered nurse (RN) licensure.[1] The certification process involves a competency-based examination that reliably assesses the candidate's abilities. To be eligible for this certification, candidates must meet several requirements. They must hold an active RN license and have a bachelor's or higher degree in nursing or a relevant field. In addition, they must have practiced the equivalent of two years full-time as a registered nurse. They must also complete 30 hours of continuing education in nursing informatics within the last three years. Lastly, they must meet specific practice hour requirements. By meeting these stringent criteria and passing the examination, nurses can demonstrate their commitment to excellence in the field of informatics nursing and enhance their professional credibility. The NI-BC certification is a testament to a nurse's dedication, expertise, and competence in the rapidly evolving field of nursing informatics.

The Certified Professional in Healthcare Information and Management Systems (CPHIMS) is a globally recognized certification offered by the Healthcare Information and Management Systems Society (HIMSS). This certification is specifically designed to assist healthcare professionals in advancing their careers by demonstrating their adherence to an international standard of professional knowledge and competence in healthcare information and management systems.[2] The eligibility requirements for this certification are quite comprehensive. Candidates must hold a baccalaureate degree and have at least five years of experience in information and management systems, with at least three of those years spent in a healthcare setting. Alternatively, candidates with a graduate degree need only three years of experience in information and management systems, provided that at least two of those years were spent in a healthcare setting. By meeting these eligibility requirements and earning the CPHIMS certification, healthcare professionals can validate their expertise and commitment to excellence in the field of healthcare information and management systems. This certification serves as a testament to their skills and dedication, enhancing their professional credibility and opening up new opportunities for career advancement.

The Certificate in Nursing Informatics (CNI) is a specialized program tailored for nurses who hold either a Bachelor of Science in Nursing (BSN) or a Master of Science in Nursing

(MSN) degree and are seeking to augment their skills in the clinical application of nursing informatics. This certificate program is typically pursued concurrently with an MSN degree, providing nurses with the opportunity to delve deeper into the field of nursing informatics. The curriculum includes additional nursing informatics courses that equip nurses with the knowledge and skills necessary to apply for certification in this specialty. By earning a CNI, nurses can demonstrate their enhanced expertise in nursing informatics. This field integrates nursing science, computer science, and information science to manage and communicate data, information, and knowledge in nursing practice. This certificate can be a significant asset for nurses aiming to leverage technology to improve patient care and outcomes.

Certifications are essential for nurses who want to specialize in informatics as they demonstrate their ability to understand and apply technology in a healthcare setting. Certifications such as the NI-BC, CPHIMS, and CNI are crucial for nurses who wish to specialize in nursing informatics. These certifications testify to a nurse's ability to understand and apply technology in healthcare. They validate the nurse's knowledge and skills in integrating nursing science with multiple information and analytical sciences to identify, define, manage, and communicate data, information, knowledge, and wisdom in nursing practice. Moreover, these certifications ensure that the nurse has met rigorous standards set by reputable credentialing bodies like the ANCC and the HIMSS. This not only enhances the nurse's professional credibility but also assures employers, colleagues, patients, and the public that the nurse is competent and skilled in nursing informatics. Obtaining these certifications often involves continuing education and practice requirements, which encourage nurses to stay updated with the latest advancements in the field of informatics. This continuous learning helps nurses to effectively use evolving technologies and informatics principles to improve patient care and outcomes.

In conclusion, certifications are more than just credentials for nurses specializing in nursing informatics. They reflect a nurse's commitment to excellence, lifelong learning, and the advancement of patient care through the effective use of technology and informatics. They are indeed a significant stepping stone in a nurse's career in the field of informatics.

Continuing Education in Nursing Informatics

In the dynamic and rapidly evolving field of healthcare technology, continuous education is not just a requirement but a necessity for nurses specializing in informatics. The healthcare landscape is constantly changing with the advent of new technologies and methodologies, making it imperative for these professionals to stay updated and adapt to these changes.

Participation in various continuing education programs and attending relevant conferences are effective ways for these nurses to stay abreast of the latest advancements in their field. These platforms provide opportunities for learning, networking, and sharing knowledge and best practices.

Organizations such as the ANA, ANCC, and HIMSS play a pivotal role. They offer many continuing education courses in nursing informatics, catering to nurses' diverse needs and interests. These courses cover a broad spectrum of subjects pertinent to nursing informatics. This includes, but is not limited to, data analytics, telehealth, and mobile health applications. Data analytics courses equip nurses with the skills to interpret and utilize healthcare data to improve patient outcomes. Telehealth courses focus on using digital information and communication technologies to access health care services remotely and manage health care. Courses on mobile health applications teach nurses about using mobile devices and apps in delivering patient care.

By pursuing continuing education, nurses specializing in informatics can enhance their knowledge and skills, thereby improving their competency and efficiency in their roles. This benefits their personal career growth and contributes to the overall improvement of patient care and outcomes in the healthcare sector. Therefore, continuous education is indeed a cornerstone for nurses in the realm of healthcare technology.

Professional Development Opportunities in Nursing Informatics

Professional development opportunities in nursing informatics offer nurses a platform to broaden their expertise and enhance their skills. These opportunities take various forms, including mentoring programs, leadership development initiatives, and research projects.

Mentoring Programs

Mentoring programs serve as a valuable resource for nurses, offering them the chance to gain insights from seasoned professionals in nursing informatics. These programs foster an environment where nurses can acquire new skills and knowledge directly from experts.

The ANI Mentoring Program is integral to their Nursing Informatics Emerging Leaders Program. This program is designed to foster the growth and development of future leaders in the field of nursing informatics. One of the unique aspects of this program is its dual mentorship approach.

Each mentee is paired with not just one but two mentors.[3] This pairing strategy is designed to counterbalance strengths and weaknesses and provide two different perspectives. Having two mentors allows the mentee to benefit from the diverse experiences, skills, and knowledge of two seasoned professionals in the field of nursing informatics. This can lead to a more comprehensive and well-rounded learning experience. For instance, one mentor might have strong technical skills, while the other might excel in leadership and management. This allows the mentee to learn and grow in multiple areas, enhancing their overall competency and preparedness for leadership roles in nursing informatics. Moreover, having two mentors can provide the mentee with a broader network and more opportunities for professional development. It also ensures that the mentee has a reliable support system throughout their journey in the program. The ANI Mentoring Program, with its dual mentorship approach, plays a crucial role in shaping future leaders in the field of nursing informatics. It provides a robust platform for learning, networking, and professional growth, thereby contributing significantly to the advancement of the field.

The ANA National Mentoring Partnership is a valuable program offered by the ANA to support nurses keen on expanding their knowledge in nursing informatics.[4] This mentoring partnership is designed to create a supportive and collaborative environment where nurses can learn from experienced professionals in nursing informatics. This program's mentors are seasoned nurses with a wealth of knowledge and experience in applying technology in healthcare settings. The mentees are nurses eager to learn and grow in nursing informatics. Through this partnership, they can interact with and learn from their mentors, gaining insights into the practical aspects of nursing informatics. The ANA National Mentoring Partnership facilitates knowledge transfer and provides a platform for professional networking. It allows mentees to connect with industry professionals, learn about the latest trends and advancements in nursing informatics, and gain a deeper understanding of the role of technology in healthcare. In essence, the ANA National Mentoring Partnership bridges theory and practice, helping nurses effectively apply their nursing informatics knowledge in real-world healthcare settings. It is a beneficial program for nurses looking to specialize in nursing informatics.

Sigma Global Nursing Excellence offers a mentoring program that is particularly beneficial for nurses interested in nursing informatics.[4] Sigma, an international nursing honor society, is known for its commitment to nursing excellence, scholarship, and leadership. Its mentoring program aligns with this commitment by providing a platform for knowledge exchange and professional development. The mentoring program pairs mentees with experienced professionals in nursing informatics. These mentors guide the mentees through their learning journey, sharing their insights, experiences, and best practices. This one-on-one interaction allows the mentees to understand nursing informatics and its practical applications better. The program provides opportunities for networking, collaboration, and career advancement. Mentees can expand their professional network by interacting with mentors and other professionals in the field, opening new opportunities for collaboration and career growth. In essence, Sigma's mentoring program is a valuable resource for nurses aiming to specialize in nursing informatics. It enhances their knowledge and skills and empowers them to excel in their careers and contribute effectively to the healthcare field.

The American Association for Nurse Practitioners (AANP) offers a mentoring program that could be particularly beneficial for nurse practitioners interested in or currently specializing in nursing informatics.[4] This mentoring program is designed to foster professional growth and development by pairing mentees with experienced nurse practitioners with a wealth of knowledge and experience in nursing informatics. These mentors provide guidance, share their insights and experiences, and help mentees navigate the complexities of the field. The program provides a supportive and collaborative environment where mentees can ask questions, discuss challenges, and learn from the practical experiences of their mentors. This interaction allows mentees to gain a deeper understanding of nursing informatics, including the application of technology in healthcare settings and the management and communication of health information. The AANP mentoring program also provides opportunities for networking and professional development. Mentees can expand their professional network by interacting with mentors and other professionals in the field, opening up new opportunities for collaboration and career advancement. The AANP mentoring program serves as a valuable resource for nurse practitioners aiming to specialize in nursing informatics.

The American Organization for Nursing Leadership (AONL) offers a mentoring program that mainly benefits nurses seeking leadership roles in nursing informatics.[4] This mentoring program is designed to foster the development of leadership skills and competencies among nurses specializing in informatics. It pairs mentees with experienced leaders in the nursing informatics field, allowing them to learn from their mentors' experiences and insights. The mentors in this program are seasoned professionals with a wealth of knowledge and experience in nursing informatics and a proven track record of leadership. They guide the mentees through their leadership journey, sharing their wisdom, and helping them navigate leadership challenges in the complex and rapidly evolving field of nursing informatics.

The AONL mentoring program also provides opportunities for networking and professional development. By interacting with mentors and other leaders in the field, mentees can expand their professional network, gain exposure to different leadership styles and strategies, and open new opportunities for career advancement. The AONL mentoring program is a valuable resource for nurses aiming to take on leadership roles in nursing informatics. It enhances their leadership skills and competencies and empowers them to lead effectively in healthcare.

Mentoring programs serve as a vital conduit for nurses, particularly those specializing in nursing informatics. These programs allow nurses to learn directly from seasoned professionals in the field, bolstering their expertise and understanding of nursing informatics. With their wealth of knowledge and experience, mentors can provide invaluable insights into the practical aspects of nursing informatics. They can guide mentees through the complexities of the field, share their experiences, and provide advice on overcoming challenges. This mentor–mentee relationship thus facilitates a deeper understanding of the field, enhances skill sets, and fosters professional growth. It is important to note that each mentoring program may offer unique advantages and have specific prerequisites. For instance, some programs focus more on technical skills, while others emphasize leadership development.

Similarly, the eligibility criteria for these programs might vary, with some requiring certain degrees or specific years of experience. Conducting comprehensive research on each program is advisable for nurses looking to specialize in nursing informatics. This research should aim to fully grasp each program's unique advantages and understand the required prerequisites. This will enable nurses to choose a program best aligned with their career goals and professional development needs. Mentoring programs are a significant resource for nurses in the field of nursing informatics. They enhance their knowledge and skills and provide them with a platform for networking and professional growth. Choosing the right program through careful research is crucial for maximizing the benefits of these programs.

Leadership Development Programs

Leadership development is crucial in helping nurses advance their careers in nursing informatics. It involves various activities designed to equip nurses with the necessary leadership skills to navigate the complexities of healthcare technology and information management. Leadership development programs often provide training in strategic thinking and decision-making. These skills are essential for nurses in informatics as they are often required to make critical decisions regarding the implementation and use of healthcare technologies. These programs also focus on communication and interpersonal skills. Effective communication is vital in nursing informatics, as professionals in this field must be able to convey complex information to various stakeholders, including other healthcare professionals, administrators, and patients. Leadership development can also involve training in change management. As nursing informatics is rapidly evolving, nurses must be able to lead and manage change effectively, ensuring that new technologies and systems are implemented smoothly and efficiently. In addition, leadership development programs often provide opportunities for networking and mentorship. Networking allows nurses to connect with other leaders in the field, learn from their experiences, and gain insights into the latest trends and advancements in nursing informatics.

Conversely, mentorship provides nurses with guidance and support from experienced professionals, helping them navigate their career paths and overcome challenges. Leadership development is a vital component of career advancement in nursing informatics. By developing leadership skills, nurses can effectively lead teams, manage change, and contribute to improving patient care by using technology and information management.

The ANI Leadership Development Program is a comprehensive program designed to cultivate leadership skills among nurses specializing in informatics. The program focuses on three key areas: developing leadership skills, providing leadership opportunities, and fostering mentor–mentee relationships.[5] Regarding leadership skills development, the program offers training and resources to help nurses enhance their strategic thinking, decision-making, and communication skills. These are crucial for leading teams, managing projects, and driving innovation in nursing informatics. The program also provides various leadership opportunities. These could range from leading a project team to participating in strategic planning and policymaking. Such opportunities allow nurses to apply their leadership skills in real-world settings, thereby gaining practical experience and enhancing their leadership competencies. The ANI Leadership Development Program places a strong emphasis on mentorship. It connects mentees with experienced leaders in the field of nursing informatics. These mentors provide guidance, share their experiences, and offer valuable insights, helping mentees navigate their career paths and overcome challenges. The ANI Leadership Development Program is a valuable platform for nurses aiming to take on leadership roles in nursing informatics. It enhances their leadership skills and provides them with opportunities to apply these skills and learn from seasoned professionals.

The American Nurses Association (ANA) Leadership Institute is a comprehensive program that provides leadership development resources for nurses at all levels, including those specializing in nursing informatics. The Leadership Institute is designed to equip nurses with the necessary leadership skills to excel in their roles and advance their careers.[6] It offers a range of resources, including online courses, webinars, and workshops, covering various aspects of nursing leadership. For nurses in nursing informatics, the Leadership Institute provides resources that are particularly relevant to their field. These resources focus on strategic decision-making in healthcare technology, managing teams in a technology-driven environment, and leading innovation in healthcare informatics. The Leadership Institute also provides opportunities for networking and mentorship. Nurses can connect with other leaders in the field, learn from their experiences, and gain insights into the latest trends and advancements in nursing informatics. The ANA Leadership Institute is a valuable platform for leadership development for nurses in nursing informatics. It enhances leadership skills and empowers nurses to lead effectively in the rapidly evolving field of healthcare technology.

The HIMSS Leadership Essentials Institute is a program designed to cultivate leadership skills among healthcare professionals, including nurses specializing in informatics. This institute offers a comprehensive set of resources and training modules that focus on the essential aspects of leadership in the context of healthcare technology and informatics.[5] The curriculum covers a wide range of topics, from strategic decision-making and team management to innovation in healthcare technology. For nurses in nursing informatics, this program provides an opportunity to learn from experienced leaders in the field. The mentors in this program share their insights and experiences, helping the mentees understand the challenges and opportunities of leading teams in a technology-driven environment. The HIMSS Leadership Essentials Institute also provides networking opportunities. By interacting with other professionals in the field, nurses can expand their professional network, gain exposure to different leadership styles and strategies, and open up new opportunities for career advancement. The HIMSS Leadership Essentials Institute is a valuable resource for nurses who want to advance in nursing informatics leadership positions. It helps them improve their leadership skills and enables them to lead successfully in the fast-changing healthcare technology domain.

The Sigma Theta Tau International Honor Society of Nursing (Sigma) Nurse Leader Academy is a program that aims to develop leadership skills among nurses, including those who specialize in nursing informatics. The Nurse Leader Academy offers a variety of resources and training modules that address the key aspects of leadership in nursing.[6] The curriculum includes topics such as strategic decision-making, team management, and innovation in healthcare. This program allows nurses in nursing informatics to learn from leaders with experience in the field. The mentors in this program provide their knowledge and perspectives, helping the mentees navigate the difficulties and opportunities of leading teams in a technology-based environment. Additionally, the Nurse Leader Academy also provides networking opportunities. By engaging with other professionals in the field, nurses can broaden their professional network, learn from different leadership styles and approaches, and discover new opportunities for their career growth. The Sigma Nurse Leader Academy is useful for nurses who want to be leaders in nursing informatics. It enables them to improve their leadership skills and equips them to lead confidently in the fast-changing field of healthcare technology.

Leadership development programs serve as a springboard for nurses to acquire knowledge from seasoned professionals in the field, thereby bolstering their leadership competencies in nursing informatics. It's highly recommended to conduct an in-depth investigation of each program to comprehend the distinct advantages they offer.

Research Programs

Research programs allow nurses to contribute to developing new technologies and practices in nursing informatics. Nurses can find opportunities to participate in research within their organizations through several avenues, including internal research programs, professional associations, policy engagement, and continuous training and education.

Internal research programs within healthcare organizations serve as a valuable resource for nurses, including those specializing in nursing informatics. These programs often involve research projects that aim to improve healthcare outcomes through innovative technology and data. Many internal research programs are conducted in partnership with academic institutions, leveraging their research expertise and resources. These collaborations often lead to cutting-edge research in nursing informatics, contributing to healthcare technology and practice advancements. Nurses interested in these research programs can reach out to their organization's research department or leadership for information about ongoing projects. This can provide them with opportunities to contribute to research initiatives, learn from experienced researchers, and stay updated on the latest trends and advancements in nursing informatics. Participation in these research programs can also enhance their professional development. It allows them to apply their informatics knowledge practically, develop research skills, and contribute to advancing nursing informatics.

Moreover, it can open new career opportunities, such as research roles or leadership positions in nursing informatics. Internal research programs offer a unique opportunity for nurses to engage in research, enhance their skills, and contribute to advancing nursing informatics. It is recommended that nurses explore these opportunities within their organizations and consider how they can contribute to and benefit from these programs.

Professional associations such as the ANA and the AANP are pivotal in advancing nursing, including nursing informatics. They often provide research opportunities that encourage nurses to contribute to the growth and development of the profession. These research opportunities often involve projects to develop new knowledge, evaluate existing practices, and apply findings to improve patient care.[7] They cover a wide range of topics pertinent to nursing, including the use of technology in healthcare, data management, patient safety, and quality of care. Participating in these research projects allows nurses to apply their informatics knowledge practically. It provides them with an opportunity to contribute to the advancement of nursing informatics, enhance their research skills, and stay updated on the latest trends and advancements in the field. These research opportunities also contribute to the professional development of nurses. They provide a platform for nurses to showcase their expertise, collaborate with other professionals, and potentially influence healthcare policies and practices. The research opportunities provided by associations like ANA and AANP are invaluable for nurses specializing in informatics. They contribute to the advancement of the nursing profession and provide nurses with opportunities for professional growth and development.

Policy engagement is a crucial aspect of nursing, particularly for those specializing in nursing informatics. It involves active participation in shaping healthcare policies that impact the profession and the quality of patient care. Nurses can engage in policy by participating in state and national nurses' associations. These associations often have committees or task forces focused on policy issues. By joining these groups, nurses can contribute their expertise, participate in policy discussions, and influence policy decisions. Attending legislative sessions is another way for nurses to engage in policy. These sessions provide insights into the legislative process and the various factors considered in policymaking. Nurses can use these opportunities to stay informed about upcoming legislation, understand its potential impact on nursing informatics, and voice their opinions. Writing white papers and policy briefs is a more direct way of influencing policy.[8] These documents provide a platform for nurses to present their research findings, share their expertise, and propose policy recommendations. By writing white papers and policy briefs, nurses can contribute to evidence-based policymaking, ensuring that the latest research and best practices in nursing informatics inform policies. Policy engagement offers a unique opportunity for nurses to shape the future of nursing informatics. By participating in nurses' associations, attending legislative sessions, and writing white papers and policy briefs, nurses can ensure that their expertise and experiences are considered in policy decisions that impact the profession and patient care.[8]

Continuing education and training programs are integral to the professional development of nurses, including those specializing in nursing informatics. These programs often encompass a variety of topics relevant to the field and frequently include research components. The research components of these programs provide nurses with an opportunity to engage in practical research activities. This could involve participating in ongoing research projects, conducting independent research, or applying research findings to their practice. Such experiences enhance their research skills and deepen their understanding of the application of research in nursing informatics.

Nurses can inquire about these opportunities through their organization's education and training department. This department typically oversees the organization's continuing education and training programs and can provide information about the availability of research opportunities. They can guide nurses on participating in these programs, the prerequisites, and the potential benefits. Participation in these programs allows nurses to stay updated on the latest trends and advancements in nursing informatics, apply their knowledge in a practical setting, and contribute to the advancement of the field. Moreover, it can open new career opportunities and enhance their professional growth (Table 9.1).

Table 9.1 Ways for Nurses to Get Involved in Policy

Ways for Nurses to Get Involved in Policy
■ Participate in state and national nurses' associations
■ Contact the advocacy or policy board of nursing associations
■ Write letters/phone state and federal officials
■ Serve on a board for the nursing association
■ Develop policy statements that affect patient care and nursing practice
■ Attend nursing association meetings and events
■ Join committees and task forces focused on policy issues
■ Engage in grassroots advocacy efforts
■ Build relationships with elected officials and policymakers
■ Stay informed about current policy issues and developments

Source: Morris G. *10 ways nurses can get involved in policy,* 2023. Retrieved from https://nursejournal.org/articles/ways-nurses-can-get-involved-in-policy/

It is essential to have a clear research interest and be proactive in seeking opportunities. It is also beneficial to network with colleagues and join professional associations, as they often provide resources and support for nurses interested in research.[7] Nurses specializing in informatics are pivotal in effectively enhancing patient care and outcomes by leveraging technology.

Conclusion

Training and education in nursing informatics are indispensable for nurses to utilize health information technologies effectively. Certifications such as the NI-BC and the CPHIMS equip nurses with the necessary knowledge and skills to excel in this field. Continuing education courses are a vital part of this learning journey. They ensure that nurses stay abreast of the latest developments in nursing informatics, a field that is rapidly evolving with advancements in technology and healthcare practices. These courses cover a wide range of topics, from data management and analytics to patient safety and quality of care, providing nurses with a comprehensive understanding of the field. Professional development opportunities further enhance this learning experience. Mentoring programs, for instance, provide nurses with a platform to learn from experienced professionals in the field. Leadership development initiatives equip them with the skills to lead teams and drive innovation in healthcare technology. Research projects allow nurses to apply their informatics knowledge in a practical setting, contributing to advancing nursing informatics. By investing in training and education in nursing informatics, nurses enhance their skills and career prospects and play a critical role in improving healthcare delivery and outcomes. The effective use of health information technologies can lead to more efficient healthcare practices, improved patient care, and, ultimately, better health outcomes.

References

1. Gaines K. *The ultimate list of nursing informatics certifications*, 2023. Retrieved from https://nurse.org/education/nursing-info rmatics-certifications/.
2. HIMSS. *CPHIMS certification*, 2023. Retrieved from www.himss. org/resources-certification/cphims.
3. ANI Mentors: Developing Tomorrow's Nursing Informatics Leaders, n.d. Retrieved November 4, 2023, from www.allianc eni.org/ani-emerging-leaders/mentors.
4. The Importance of Mentorship in Nursing, n.d. Retrieved November 4, 2023, from https://nursejournal.org/resources/the-importance-of-mentorship-in-nursing/.
5. Handzel S. *Supporting nurse informatics leadership development*, 2022. Retrieved from www.wolterskluwer.com/ en/expert-insights/supporting-nurse-informatics-leadership-development.
6. Backonja U, Mook P, Langford LH. Calling nursing informatics leaders: opportunities for personal and professional growth, *Online J Issues Nurs*, 2021.
7. Altman M. *Why should I participate in nursing research?* 2020. Retrieved from www.aacn.org/blog/why-should-i-participate-in-nursing-research.
8. Morris G. *10 ways nurses can get involved in policy*, 2023. Retrieved from https://nursejournal.org/articles/ways-nurses-can-get-involved-in-policy/.

Chapter 10

Future of Nursing Informatics

Importance of Nursing Informatics in Healthcare

Nursing informatics is a dynamic field that combines nursing science, computer science, and information science. Nursing informatics is crucial in managing and communicating data, information, knowledge, and wisdom within clinical practice.[1] Nursing informatics is currently at the forefront of transforming healthcare. The role of nursing informatics in healthcare is pivotal and supports consumers, patients, nurses, and healthcare providers in decision-making across all roles and settings. Nursing informatics professionals work with diverse stakeholders across the care continuum, helping to bridge the gap between clinical and technical perspectives.[2]

Nurse informaticists have an essential role in shaping clinical workflow and helping to enhance productivity and quality of care. For instance, during the COVID-19 pandemic, nursing informatics specialists played a crucial role in

166

establishing new clinical workflows, increasing operational efficiencies, and improving care quality for their patients.[3]

The specialty transforms raw data into valuable information and utilizes technology to enhance health and healthcare equity, safety, quality, and outcomes. Nursing informatics is broad, covering the design, development, implementation, and evaluation of effective informatics solutions and technologies within practice's clinical, administrative, educational, and research domains.[1] Administratively, it enhances processes through technology. In the educational realm, it supports nursing education and training. Additionally, nursing informatics is crucial in research by leveraging informatics tools for data analysis, optimization, and evidence-based practice.

Nurse informaticists play a pivotal role in healthcare by facilitating efficient and accurate communication of patient information among healthcare providers. Their work improves care coordination and patient safety, enables healthcare providers to make evidence-based decisions and interventions, and improves patient outcomes. Furthermore, nurse informaticists contribute to the development of patient-centered care by promoting patients' access to their health records and empowering them to participate in their care.

As the field of nursing informatics evolves, there is a growing need for informatics nurses to consider graduate-level preparation to assume the role of informatics nurse specialists. These specialists support operations as project managers, analysts, and department leaders.

Since its emergence in the 1960s, nursing informatics has evolved significantly.[4] It now encompasses various activities, such as developing electronic health records, clinical decision support systems, telehealth, and patient monitoring systems. Recognized as a nursing specialty by the American Nurses Association, it has its certification, competencies, scope, and standards of practice.[5] Nursing informatics is pivotal in transforming healthcare through technology and data-driven practices, from designing and implementing effective informatics solutions to advocating for policy development. Nursing informatics will be a critical factor in healthcare in the future, with progress focusing on automated records of patient and clinical data, enhanced operations at healthcare facilities, more accessible data collection, tracking, and analysis, and immediate access to patient information.

Emerging Trends in Nursing Informatics

Digital Health

Digital health is a significant transformation in healthcare, characterized by using digital technologies for various health-related purposes. This trend is changing how healthcare is provided, making it more convenient, efficient, and personalized. As digital health grows, nurse informaticists and nurses must be vital in this change.

Nurses at the front line of patient care are uniquely positioned to influence the research and development of digital health technologies. Their knowledge of patient needs, and the complexities of healthcare delivery can inspire innovation that is both useful and beneficial for patient outcomes. Additionally, nurses' involvement in the design process ensures that these technologies are easy to use and adapted to the workflows of healthcare providers.

Digital health tools also depend on nurses, who must be skilled at using and incorporating these technologies into their daily practice. Their engagement is vital for effectively implementing digital systems, such as electronic health records, telehealth services, or mobile health applications.

Therefore, educational programs and continuous training are essential to prepare nurses with digital literacy skills.

Moreover, nurses must actively use new digital technologies to improve their practice and advocate for their patients. Nurses can contribute to better health outcomes, more efficient disease management, and a better patient healthcare experience by leveraging data analytics, artificial intelligence (AI), and other advanced tools.

The growth of digital health is not just a technological change but a cultural one that requires the active involvement of nursing professionals. Their participation is crucial in ensuring that digital health technologies are effectively researched, designed, used, and maximized to their full potential, ultimately leading to a more sophisticated and human-centered healthcare system.

Cloud Technology

The cloud-first approach is a strategic framework healthcare organizations use to prioritize cloud computing services for data management and healthcare delivery. This paradigm shift is motivated by the need for more accessibility and scalability in healthcare operations.[6] By transferring data and services to the cloud, healthcare providers can enjoy cloud platforms' flexibility and efficiency.

One of the main advantages of the cloud-first approach is accessibility. Healthcare professionals can access patient data and vital applications from anywhere, at any time, as long as they have internet connectivity. This is especially useful for remote patient monitoring and telemedicine, which need real-time access to patient information to provide timely care.

Another essential benefit is scalability. Cloud services can be easily scaled up or down depending on the demand, allowing healthcare organizations to manage resources more effectively. During periods of high demand, such as a public health crisis, the cloud can handle the increase in data traffic and service requests without the need for significant infrastructure investments.

Furthermore, the cloud-first approach enables collaboration among healthcare professionals. With data stored in a centralized location, multiple users can work on same documents or access same information simultaneously, improving care coordination.

Cloud services also improve data security and compliance, with regulations such as Health Insurance Portability and Accountability Act (HIPAA) are also improved through cloud services. Reliable cloud providers invest heavily in security measures to protect sensitive health information against breaches and cyber threats.

Additionally, the cloud-first strategy supports the integration of advanced analytics and AI.[6] These technologies can analyze large amounts of data to provide insights for personalized medicine, predictive analytics, and decision support systems. The cloud-first approach is transforming healthcare by providing a strong, secure, and flexible infrastructure that supports the dynamic needs of the healthcare industry. It allows healthcare organizations to leverage technological advancements to improve patient care, streamline operations, and foster innovation in the healthcare ecosystem.

Artificial Intelligence (AI)

Artificial intelligence (AI) is poised to transform healthcare, creating new possibilities to enhance patient care. AI is a versatile tool that can significantly improve patient outcomes by providing more precise diagnoses, tailored treatment plans, and predictive analytics that can forecast health events before they happen. The quality of care is also set to improve through AI's ability to quickly process and analyze large amounts of data. This can lead to more informed decision-making and a decrease in human error. For example, AI algorithms can help interpret medical images with higher accuracy, thus supporting radiologists in spotting anomalies sooner and more reliably.[7]

Efficiency is another area where AI offers substantial improvements. By automating routine tasks like data entry and patient scheduling, AI can allow healthcare professionals to concentrate more on direct patient care activities. This not only optimizes the use of resources but also lowers the risk of burnout among healthcare staff.

For nurse informaticists, incorporating AI into healthcare poses both opportunities and challenges. Ethical considerations are essential when it comes to AI deployment. Issues such as data privacy, consent, and the potential for bias in AI algorithms must be carefully addressed to maintain trust and uphold the standards of patient care.

Furthermore, the rapid development of AI technologies requires a commitment to ongoing education and professional development. Nurse informaticists must keep up with the latest developments and understand how to apply them effectively in healthcare. This includes being skilled in data science and analytics and having a solid understanding of the ethical and legal implications of AI.

In short, AI is not just a technological innovation but a driver for a more responsive, effective, and patient-centered healthcare system. Nurse informaticists are vital to achieving this potential as they connect clinical practice and technological innovation. Their role in guiding the ethical use of AI, advocating for patient rights, and fostering a culture of continuous learning will be crucial in shaping the future of healthcare.

Big Data

Big data management in healthcare involves the process of acquiring, storing, analyzing, and using large amounts of health-related data to enhance patient care and operational efficiency.[8] Nurse informaticists have a profound impact in this domain, as they ensure that big data aligns with the goal of improving patient outcomes and streamlining healthcare delivery. They have a vital role in managing big data by applying their clinical expertise and informatics skills to interpret and use data effectively. They examine patterns, trends, and similarities among patient populations to guide clinical decisions, prevent disease, and promote health. By doing this, they help develop evidence-based practices that improve patient care.

The ethical management of big data is also a significant issue for nurse informaticists. They must ensure patient data is treated with the highest confidentiality and security, following regulations such as HIPAA. Moreover, they advocate for the appropriate use of data, ensuring that algorithms and analytics are free from bias and serve the interests of all patient groups.

Nurse informaticists are at the forefront of integrating big data with patient care. They help create and implement information systems that support healthcare providers in making data-driven decisions. This includes using electronic health records (EHRs), clinical decision support systems (CDSSs), and other digital tools that improve the reliability and efficiency of care delivery.

In conclusion, managing big data in healthcare is a complicated and critical task that requires nurse informaticists' specialized knowledge and skills. Their impact is felt across the healthcare spectrum, from improving patient outcomes and care quality to ensuring ethical data use and contributing to the financial health of care organizations.

Internet of Medical Things

Internet of medical things (IoMT) is an emerging healthcare field involving a network of connected devices that collect, transmit, and analyze health data.[9] This technology enhances the healthcare sector by improving patient care, facilitating disease management, and optimizing healthcare operations.

Nurse informaticists are crucial for the effective implementation of IoMT in healthcare settings. Their role involves understanding and handling the intersection of patient care, information systems, and IoMT devices. They ensure these technologies are used productively to support health outcomes and align with clinical workflows.

IoMT devices include wearable fitness trackers and advanced sensors that measure vital signs.[9] They enable continuous patient monitoring, which can help detect potential health issues and provide timely interventions. This real-time data collection enables a more preventive approach to patient care.

Nurse informaticists are responsible for managing the large amounts of data generated by IoMT devices. They use their skills to analyze this data, derive valuable insights, and inform clinical decision-making. This can result in personalized care plans and increased patient engagement.

IoMT also presents challenges, such as maintaining data privacy and security. Nurse informaticists must address these issues, ensure adherence to HIPAA regulations, and promote ethical data usage standards.

Nurse informaticists have a vital role in educating healthcare staff about IoMT. They advocate for adopting these technologies and provide training to ensure that healthcare providers are proficient in using IoMT devices effectively.

The future of IoMT in healthcare is promising, with the potential for even more integration into patient care. Nurse informaticists will continue to be key players in advancing IoMT, driving innovation, and shaping the future of digital healthcare.

Remote Patient Monitoring

Remote patient monitoring (RPM) in healthcare is a system that uses digital technologies to gather and send medical and other health data from patients remotely.[10] This data is then electronically shared with healthcare providers for evaluation, recommendations, and, if needed, interventions. RPM is beneficial for managing chronic conditions, post-discharge care, and preventive health measures.

The role of nurse informaticists in the field of RPM is significant. They are essential in implementing and optimizing RPM technologies, ensuring that these tools are integrated smoothly into the healthcare delivery system. Nurse informaticists examine the data gathered through RPM, helping to make informed clinical decisions that enhance patient care. They also play a vital role in training other healthcare professionals on how to use RPM technologies efficiently.

RPM enables patients in remote or underserved areas to receive high-quality care without frequent travel to healthcare facilities. Continuous monitoring can lead to early identification of potential health issues, allowing for timely intervention and better disease management. By reducing the need for in-person visits, RPM can lower healthcare costs and improve the utilization of healthcare resources.

Cybersecurity Measures

Cybersecurity measures are essential for the quality of healthcare services and the protection of patient data. As healthcare systems rely increasingly on digital technologies, nurse informaticists are vital in ensuring and improving cybersecurity.

Nurse informaticists contribute to developing and implementing cybersecurity policies and strategies because they have a deep understanding of clinical workflows and patient care processes. They are often the first to spot potential cybersecurity issues and weaknesses within healthcare settings.[11]

Their knowledge is crucial for designing training programs that match the actual workflow experiences of nursing staff, leading to better engagement and compliance with security protocols. Training can be customized to nurses' real-world situations, making it more relevant and relatable. Nurse informaticists may participate in cybersecurity incident response exercises, helping plan and coordinate the healthcare organization's response to cyber events.

They ensure that all remote monitoring and digital communication follow regulatory standards such as HIPAA, protecting patient privacy and data security. Nurse informaticists evaluate new technologies for potential cybersecurity risks before using them in healthcare settings.

They advocate for including nursing perspectives in cybersecurity discussions at the organizational level, ensuring that nursing's unique needs are considered. This highlights the critical role that nurse informaticists play in the intersection of healthcare and cybersecurity.

The Future of Nursing Informatics

The future of nursing informatics is poised to be influenced by several factors, including technological advancements, healthcare policies, and societal trends. Technological advancements such as AI, machine learning, and big data analytics are anticipated to significantly shape the evolution of nursing informatics.[12] These technologies can assist in analyzing vast amounts of data, thereby enabling healthcare professionals to make informed decisions and provide patient care.

Healthcare policies, especially those related to data privacy and interoperability, will also substantially impact the future of nursing informatics. As healthcare increasingly digitizes, policies ensuring the secure and efficient health information exchange will become more crucial.[13]

Societal trends, such as the growing emphasis on patient-centered care and health equity, are also expected to shape the future of nursing informatics. Nursing informatics will likely play a pivotal role in addressing social determinants of health and advancing health equity.[13]

As the field continues to evolve, nursing informatics professionals will be at the forefront of leveraging technology to improve patient care and health outcomes. This comprehensive approach makes nursing informatics an indispensable part of the future of healthcare.

Preparing for the Future

Nursing informatics professionals need to have a combination of clinical, technological, and collaborative skills to adapt to the changing healthcare environment. They require strong analytical and critical thinking skills and solid problem-solving abilities. These skills will help nurse informaticists to understand complex health data and find practical solutions to healthcare issues. They will also need experience with health data systems and information technology skills. This technical knowledge will enable nurse informaticists to manage and use health information systems efficiently and modify or create software solutions.

Collaboration in multidisciplinary teams requires interpersonal skills such as conflict resolution, empathy, flexibility, and teamwork. These skills enable diverse healthcare professionals to communicate and cooperate effectively, ensuring that informatics solutions are aligned with healthcare workflows. Moreover, technical skills and the capacity to quickly adjust to new technologies and innovations will be crucial. Nursing informatics is changing rapidly, with new technologies and practices constantly evolving. Nurse informaticists will have to keep up with these changes and be able to acquire and use new tools and techniques swiftly.

Finally, future nurse informaticists need strong project management skills to lead and manage informatics projects. They should be able to plan and coordinate tasks, manage resources, track progress, and finish projects on time and within budget. These skills and abilities will help them use information and technology to improve healthcare.

Strategies for Integrating Future Trends into Nursing Practice

Nursing professionals can adopt several strategies to integrate future trends into their practice and improve patient care. First, they should engage in lifelong learning and continuing professional development to stay updated with technological advancements. This includes participating in workshops, seminars, and online courses focusing on emerging technologies in healthcare. Second, they should collaborate with other healthcare professionals and learn from their experiences. This can be achieved through interdisciplinary team meetings and case discussions. Nurse informaticists are crucial in fostering collaboration within healthcare settings, translating the technical and operational requirements of virtual care, and implementing system solutions. Third, they should actively participate in designing and implementing new technologies in their practice settings. This will ensure that the technologies are tailored to meet the specific needs of their patients and improve care delivery. Nurse informaticists have a massive opportunity to assess the inputs and outputs of emerging technologies in clinical settings, ensuring their safe application in care delivery. Fourth, they should advocate for policies that support technology integration in healthcare. This includes policies that address data privacy, interoperability, and the ethical use of technology. Balancing innovation with ethical standards is essential for building trust in AI-driven healthcare solutions. Lastly, they should leverage technology to promote patient-centered care. This includes using telehealth to provide care to patients in remote areas, using EHRs to personalize care, and using predictive analytics to improve patient outcomes (Table 10.1).

Conclusion

To sum up, nursing informatics is a vibrant and continually evolving discipline that holds a significant position in the healthcare sector. It merges the principles of nursing science, computer science, and information science to manage and disseminate data, information, knowledge, and wisdom within

Table 10.1   Strategies for Integrating Future Trends into Nursing Practice

Strategy	Description
Lifelong Learning and Continuing Professional Development	Nursing professionals should continually learn and develop professionally to keep up with technological advancements, which includes participating in various educational activities focused on emerging healthcare technologies.
Collaboration	Nursing professionals should foster collaboration with peers, learning from shared experiences and interdisciplinary discussions. Nurse informaticists are key in this process, facilitating collaboration, translating technical requirements, and implementing solutions.
Active Participation in Design and Implementation of New Technologies	Nursing professionals should be actively involved in designing and implementing new technologies in their practice, ensuring they meet patient needs and enhance care. Nurse informaticists play a key role in evaluating and safely applying these emerging technologies in clinical settings.
Advocacy for Policies Supporting Technology Integration	Nursing professionals should champion policies that facilitate healthcare technology integration, addressing data privacy, interoperability, and ethical use. Striking a balance between innovation and ethics is crucial for building trust in AI-driven healthcare.
Leveraging Technology to Promote Patient-Centered Care	Nursing professionals should utilize technology to enhance patient-centered care, including telehealth for remote patients, electronic health records for personalized care, and predictive analytics to improve outcomes.

clinical practice. The contribution of nursing informatics to healthcare is vital, aiding consumers, patients, nurses, and healthcare providers in decision-making across all roles and environments.

Professionals in nursing informatics collaborate with a wide range of stakeholders throughout the care continuum, bridging clinical and technical viewpoints. They shape clinical workflows, boost productivity, and enhance the quality of care. This specialty transforms raw data into useful information and employs technology to improve health and healthcare equity, safety, quality, and outcomes.

As this field progresses, professionals in nursing informatics will lead the way in utilizing technology to enhance patient care and health outcomes. This holistic approach positions nursing informatics as an essential component of the future of healthcare. The trajectory of nursing informatics will be shaped by various factors, including technological advancements, healthcare policies, and societal trends.

Nursing informatics professionals must possess clinical, technological, and collaborative skills to adapt to the evolving healthcare landscape. They need robust analytical and critical thinking skills and solid problem-solving abilities. These skills will enable nurse informaticists to comprehend complex health data and devise practical solutions to healthcare challenges.

In the wake of swift technological advancements and changing practices, the significance of lifelong learning, technological expertise, adaptability, and ethical vigilance in the ever-changing field of nursing informatics cannot be emphasized enough. Despite the challenges, these advancements in informatics are laying the groundwork for more efficient and effective patient care, highlighting the importance of nursing informatics in the transformation of healthcare.

References

1. Gaines K. *What is nursing informatics?*, 2023. Retrieved from https://nurse.org/resources/nursing-informatics/.
2. What Is Nursing Informatics?, February 27, 2023. Retrieved from www.himss.org/resources/what-nursing-informatics.
3. Schoenbaum A. *Nursing informatics key role in defining clinical workflow, increasing efficiency and improving quality*, September 30, 2020. Retrieved from www.himss.org/resources/nursing-informatics-key-role-defining-clinical-workflow-increasing-efficiency-and.
4. Sweeney J. Healthcare informatics. Online J Nursing Inform. 2017;21(1).
5. American Nurses Association. *Nursing Informatics: Scope and Standards of Practice*. 3rd ed. Silver Spring, MD: American Nurses Association, 2022.
6. Cresswell K, Domínguez Hernández A, Williams R, Sheikh A. Key challenges and opportunities for cloud technology in health care: semistructured interview study. JMIR Human Fact. 2022;9(1):e31246. https://doi.org/10.2196/31246.
7. Syed A, Zoga A. Artificial intelligence in radiology: current technology and future directions. Sem Musculoskel Radiol. 2018;22(05):540–545. https://doi.org/10.1055/s-0038-1673383.
8. Dash S, Shakyawar SK, Sharma M, Kaushik S. Big data in healthcare: management, analysis and future prospects. J Big Data. 2019;6(1):54. https://doi.org/10.1186/s40537-019-0217-0.
9. Kelly JT, Campbell KL, Gong E, Scuffham P. The internet of things: impact and implications for health care delivery. J Med Internet Res. 2020;22(11):e20135. https://doi.org/10.2196/20135.
10. Schultz M. Telehealth and remote patient monitoring innovations in nursing practice: state of the science. Online J Issues Nurs. 2023;28(2). https://doi.org/10.3912/OJIN.Vol28No02ST01.
11. Kamerer JL, McDermott D. Cybersecurity: nurses on the front line of prevention and education. J Nurs Regul. 2020;10(4):48–53. https://doi.org/10.1016/S2155-8256(20)30014-4.

12. Booth RG, Strudwick G, McBride S, O'Connor S, Solano López AL. How the nursing profession should adapt for a digital future. BMJ. 2021;373:n1190. https://doi.org/10.1136/bmj.n1190

13. Future of Nursing: Nursing Informatics Industry Perspectives, May 4, 2023. Retrieved from www.himss.org/resources/future-nursing-nursing-informatics-industry-perspectives.

Index

Note: Page locators in **bold** and *italics* represents tables and figures, respectively.

Printed in the United States
by Baker & Taylor Publisher Services